MORALITY

— OF —

THE SABBATH

BY

ELD. D. M. CANRIGHT.

------>◇<------

STEAM PRESS
OF THE SEVENTH-DAY ADVENTIST PUBLISHING ASSOCIATION.
BATTLE CREEK, MICH.:
1875.

PRINTED IN
THE UNITED STATES OF AMERICA

World rights reserved. This book or any portion thereof may not be copied or reproduced in any form or manner whatever, except as provided by law, without the written permission of the publisher, except by a reviewer who may quote brief passages in a review.

The author assumes full responsibility for the accuracy
of all facts and quotations as cited in this book.

Facsimile Reproduction

As this book played a formative role in the development of Christian thought and the publisher feels that this book, with its candor and depth, still holds significance for the church today. Therefore the publisher has chosen to reproduce this historical classic from an original copy. Frequent variations in the quality of the print are unavoidable due to the condition of the original. Thus the print may look darker or lighter or appear to be missing detail, more in some places than in others.

2006 07 08 09 10 11 12 · 5 4 3 2 1

Copyright © 2006 TEACH Services, Inc.
ISBN-13: 978-1-57258-400-6
ISBN-10: 1-57258-400-9
Library of Congress Control Number: 2006920047

Published by
TEACH Services, Inc.
www.TEACHServices.com

PREFACE.

The object of this Pamphlet is to show that the seventh-day Sabbath of the decalogue is of equal importance with the other precepts of that holy law; that, like them, it is moral in its nature, and, hence properly belongs in the moral law where God has placed it; and that when the Sabbath is considered in all its bearings, it is all-important as a constantly-recurring test of man's love and loyalty to his Creator.

Hoping that God will bless these pages to the honor of his name, the vindication of his holy Sabbath, and the salvation of souls, I commend it to his good providence.

D. M. C.

OAKLAND, CAL., AUGUST, 1875.

THE MORALITY OF THE SABBATH.

When the claims of God's holy Sabbath are presented, and its observance is urged upon the people, then every effort is made by its opponents to belittle it as an institution of small account. It is said that the Sabbath law is only a ceremonial precept, given simply for man's convenience, and that its observance or non-observance is a matter of little importance. While it is admitted that all the other precepts of the decalogue are moral and their observance all-important, it is asserted that the fourth commandment is of a very different nature, containing no test of moral character. The only importance attached to it is that of a day for physical rest and religious gatherings.

While the Sabbath is regarded in this light, of course men will not feel very particular about observing it. We propose, therefore, to show that the nature and design of God's Sabbath day is as much higher than this view of it as Heaven is higher than the earth; that it is not only a moral institution, but that it is the most important precept in the whole decalogue. In proof that the Sabbath is a moral precept, we offer the following facts:—

I. *Moral duties and precepts are such as grow out of the attributes of God. Creative power is the distinguishing attribute of the living God, and the Sabbath grew directly out of the exercise of this attribute in the creation of the world.*

I do not see how the truthfulness of this proposition can be denied by any one. Why are we morally bound to serve God ? Because he created us and all the blessings which we enjoy. None will deny that this is the basis of all our duties to God. A little reflection will show that it is not so much the wisdom, or the justice, or the holiness, or any other attribute, of the Deity, as it is his act of creating us, which makes it our moral duty to obey him. Notwithstanding God is infinitely wise, just, holy, &c., could we bring ourselves into existence and sustain ourselves without his aid, we would be under no obligation to serve him. This is an important fact which we wish the reader to weigh carefully. It is, then, God's attribute of creative power above all others, that is the basis of all our moral duties to him. He made us by his power as a Creator, and by his power he can destroy us; hence he has a perfect right to say what we shall, or shall not, do. So Paul argues in Rom. 9 : 20–23. Now the very basis of the Sabbath was God's act of creating the world in six days and resting upon the seventh. "Remember the Sabbath day, to keep it holy . . . . . For in six days the Lord made heaven and earth, the sea, and all that in them is, and rested the seventh day; wherefore [for this reason] the Lord blessed the Sabbath day and hallowed it." Ex. 20:8-11; Gen. 2:1-3.

The foundation of the Sabbatic precept, then, is the same as that of all other moral precepts; and hence it must be moral.

II. *The Sabbath, like all other moral precepts, rests upon eternal and unalterable facts.*

In creating the world, God worked the first six days of the first week of time. He then rested upon the seventh day. That act made it his rest-day, or Sabbath day. *Sabbath* is a Hebrew word signifying *rest*. Hence, the Sabbath day of the Lord signifies the rest-day of the Lord. Therefore, when God had rested upon the seventh day, that day had thus become distinguished from all the other days of the week as God's *rest*, or *Sabbath*, day. When a man is born upon a certain day, that day becomes his *birthday*. No other day in the year is his birthday. So the day upon which God rested, the seventh day, and no other, is God's Sabbath day.

These facts of creation are just as true now as they were when the Sabbath was first given, six thousand years ago. Is it not as true now as it was then that God did work the first six days of the week? Certainly. Then these are still only working days, as the Lord has properly named them. "Thus saith the Lord God, The gate of the inner court that looketh toward the east shall be shut the *six working days;* but on the Sabbath it shall be opened." Eze. 46:1. Is it not also just as true now as it was then that the seventh day is God's Sabbath day? Is it not still the day upon which he rested, and, hence, his rest-day? Can you change your birthday from the day upon which you were born to one upon which you were not born? Of course not. Neither can the Lord's rest-day be changed from the day upon which he did rest to one upon which he did not rest. Has the first day of the week become the Sabbath (rest) day of the Lord? Impossible, because no day can become God's rest-day till he has first rested upon that day. But God never did rest upon any day except the seventh. Hence, the Sabbath day of the Lord is unchangeably fixed to the seventh day. This will always remain a fixed fact while the earth stands, which will be eternally. For this earth is to be purified and become the everlasting abode of the righteous. Isa. 65:17–25; 2 Pet. 3:7–13; Isa. 66:22, 23. So long as days shall continue to succeed each other, so long must the seventh day continue to be the Creator's Sabbath day. And so we read in Isa. 66:22, 23: "For as the new heavens and the new earth, which I will make, shall remain before me, saith the Lord, so shall your seed and your name remain. And it shall come to pass, that from one new moon to another, and *from one Sabbath to another*, shall all flesh come to worship before me, saith the Lord." This evidence proves my proposition true, that the Sabbath is founded upon unchange-

OF THE SABBATH.

able and eternal facts, the same as all moral precepts are. Here, also, it seems to me that all must admit the truthfulness of this proposition.

III. *The principle of every moral precept existed before the fall, and would have existed if man had never fallen. This is true of the Sabbath. But all ceremonial precepts were introduced after the fall, to shadow forth redemption.*

Here again we find that true of the Sabbath which is true of all moral commandments, viz., that it was a primary institution existing before the fall of man. But this is not true of any ceremonial statute. Idolatry, image worship, profanity, lying, stealing, &c., would all have been as morally wrong if committed before the fall as after. Hence, moral duties may be defined as those resting upon primary principles, or those which did exist before man fell, or before any remedial system was instituted. Ceremonial precepts are those which came in consequence of the fall, and which would never have existed but for sin. They grew out of the creature's action as a sinner, and shadowed forth his coming redemption. This is a plainly marked and undeniable distinction between moral and ceremonial precepts. Now we only have to ask to which of these two classes the Sabbath belongs, in order to determine whether it is a moral or a ceremonial precept.

Only one answer can be given to this. Every fact and principle upon which the Sabbath ever was based did exist before Adam sinned. Creation's work was ended, and the Lord's rest upon the seventh day was in the past. God had placed his blessing upon the seventh day and had set it apart to a sacred use. Thus the record reads: "Thus the heavens and the earth were finished, and all the host of them. And on the seventh day God ended his work which he had made; and he rested on the seventh day from all his work which he had made. And God blessed the seventh day, and sanctified it; because that in it he had rested from all his work which God created and made." Gen. 2:1-3.

This is a plain, chronological narration of what occurred in Eden. God worked six days, rested the seventh day, blessed it, and then sanctified it. Sanctify is thus defined by Webster: "To separate, set apart, or appoint, to a holy or religious use." Then the Lord did set apart to a holy use the seventh day in Eden. Every reference afterward to the origin of the Sabbath points back to Eden. See Ex. 16:23; 20:8-11; 31:17; Mark 2:27. The Sabbath is a memorial of creation, as I will soon show; and hence became necessary as soon as creation week was ended. But for what were types, and shadows, and ceremonies? To point to redemption through Christ who was to come. Col. 2:17; Heb. 10:1. But these were not given until man needed redemption; and he did not need redemption till after he had sinned. But the Sabbath was given before man sinned, and hence was not a typical or ceremonial institution. So we find that the Sabbath is a primary institution, all the reasons for which, like those for every moral precept, existed before the fall. The following established principle in law applies in this case: "Where there is no law by statute, but a *reason* for such law exists, the law itself is presumed to be in force." —*Broom's Legal Maxims*.

Every fact and reason upon which the Sabbath was founded did exist before man fell in Eden. Hence the record in Gen. 2:1–3, which says that God made, blessed, and set apart, the Sabbath day in Eden, is true and reasonable. Hence it cannot be typical or ceremonial.

IV. *Man's moral duty to love and obey God rests chiefly upon the fact that the Lord created all things, which fact the Sabbath was given to commemorate.*

God made me and all the blessings that surround me, hence it is my moral duty to love and serve him as the Author and Giver of them all. Those who do not believe that God created the world feel under no obligation to obey him, even if they believe that there is a God at all, which they seldom do. Hence it becomes of the greatest importance, morally, that the facts of creation be ever kept fresh in the memory of men. If these facts be disbelieved or forgotten, the Creator himself will also be forgotten.

Man is constantly prone to forget his Creator and to deny his existence. To have, to preserve, and to teach, the knowledge of the true God is the very highest of all moral duties. Indeed, without this we could not serve God at all. How morally important, then, that God should give men something which would be a frequent and constant reminder of the Creator and of our obligation to him. For just this purpose God did give the Sabbath to man in the very beginning. Thus we read, "And God blessed the seventh day, and sanctified it [why?]; *because* that in it he had rested from all his work which God created and made." Gen. 2:3. A rest implies a work performed. God had just finished the wonderful work of creation, on account of which "the morning stars sang together, and all the sons of God shouted for joy." Job 38:7. As a monument for a memorial of this great work, God there set apart the seventh day to be a sacred rest. From that time on through all ages the observance of the Creator's rest-day was to be a weekly reminder, or memorial, of God's work of creating the heavens and the earth. Every time a person intelligently keeps the Sabbath day it reminds him of God's work of creating the earth at the beginning in six days and resting upon the seventh day. Thus it is an appropriate memorial of creation.

When the Lord gives the reason for the observance of the Sabbath, he always points back to the facts of creation. Thus, when he gave the decalogue from Mount Sinai, the Lord said, "Remember the Sabbath day, to keep it holy. Six days shalt thou labor, and do all thy work; but the seventh day is the Sabbath of the Lord thy God; in it thou shalt not do any work [why? for what reason?]; . . . *for* in six days the Lord made heaven and earth, the sea, and all that in them is, and rested the seventh day; wherefore the Lord blessed the Sabbath day, and hallowed it." Ex. 20 : 8–11. Why was the Sabbath hallowed? Because God had rested upon it after his six days of labor at creation.

A sign and a memorial are the same thing. The 4th chapter of Joshua proves this, while at the same time it gives us a beautiful illustration of the use of a memorial, or sign. When the children of Israel crossed over Jordan, the waters of the river were cut off and dried up. Then the Lord directed them to take twelve stones out of the bottom of Jordan, and make an heap of them upon the bank of the river, "that this may be a *sign* among you, that when your children ask their fathers in time to come, saying, What mean ye by these stones? Then ye shall answer them, That the waters of Jordan were cut off before the ark of the covenant of the Lord; when it passed over Jordan, the waters of Jordan were cut off; and these stones shall be for a *memorial* unto the children of Israel forever." Josh. 4 : 6, 7. The Lord says that these stones shall be a *sign* among you; and then he says they shall be a *memorial*, showing that sign and memorial were synonymous.

When the Lord explains the object of the sign,

or memorial, he says that when their children in days to come ask their fathers what these stones mean, then the fathers shall tell them the story of the way in which the waters of Jordan were cut off, &c., when their fathers passed over Jordan. Thus, in all coming generations, whenever men looked upon this pile of stones it would constantly remind them of that wonderful miracle which God wrought for his people, and thus keep it fresh in the memory. So God declares that the Sabbath is a sign of creation. "Wherefore the children of Israel shall keep the Sabbath, to observe the Sabbath throughout their generations, for a perpetual covenant. It is a *sign* between me and the children of Israel forever [how? and why?]; *for* in six days the Lord made heaven and earth, and on the seventh day he rested, and was refreshed." Ex. 31:16, 17. Here the Lord directly says that the Sabbath is a *sign*. We have already shown that sign and memorial are synonymous. But why is it a sign? The reason is plainly stated. "*For in six days the Lord made heaven and earth, and on the seventh day he rested.*" Thus the Sabbath is declared to be a divinely appointed memorial of God's great work of creation. Its importance cannot be overestimated. God instituted it for a great moral purpose, namely, to preserve in the memory of men a knowledge of his work of creation.

Had the human family carefully observed this sacred memorial, they never would have forgotten the living God and have become atheists or the worshipers of false gods.

"Had all men properly kept the Sabbath, all would have known Jehovah and worshiped him from the creation of the world to the present time, and idolatry never would have been practiced on the earth."—*Justin Edwards.*

The Sabbath, therefore, does have for its object the greatest of all moral principles, namely, the preservation in the earth of the knowledge of the true and living God, the Creator of the earth. The reader cannot fail to observe that, if this be so, the farther we come from creation the more important becomes the careful observance of the Sabbath. For during the first few generations, the facts of creation might have been handed down from father to son without any memorial. But now, when all such traditional knowledge has been lost, and men are becoming skeptical with regard to God's existence and the miraculous work of creation, how morally important becomes the preservation of the ancient and divinely-instituted memorial of creation, God's holy rest-day!

V. *Man's nature, physically and mentally, requires just such a day of rest as the Sabbath precept provides, and hence, like all moral precepts, it provides for a natural and universal want of the race.*

Moral precepts are those which grow out of the nature of things, those which are founded upon the attributes of God and the nature of man. The Sabbath precept looks both ways—to God and to man—and may be said to be doubly moral from that fact. That man's physical nature requires just such a rest-day as the Sabbath, is susceptible of the clearest proof. This, man's experience for six thousand years has abundantly proved. A volume might be written upon this one point without exhausting the subject. We have room for only a few brief statements.

Experiments have been tried in various ways, and careful observations have been taken, all going to show that both men and animals will accomplish more labor in a given time, do it in a better manner, and preserve better health, by resting every seventh day, than they will by working continuously. Where men or animals work day after day continuously, without a regular, weekly day of rest, they soon become worn down, jaded out, depressed in spirit, slack in their habits, and every way unfitted for earnest, careful, cheerful labor. Experiments with horses on street cars and canal boats have been tried; with men on railroads, in mills, mines, and other places; and everywhere the same results have followed.

Two mills with the same machinery, capital, hands, &c., have run side by side for a year, one working six days and the other seven days in the week. The one running six days accomplished more work, and did it in a better manner, than the one running seven days. Travelers over the Plains have observed similar results. The testimonies which follow, all witness to the truth that man's physical and mental nature needs rest, just such a rest as the Sabbath institution affords. Though some of them refer to a day not the Sabbath—a day not sanctified and commanded by Jehovah—they are evidence in regard to the necessity of a Sabbath. But man's physical requirements are and should be subservient to the moral; and his moral requirements must have respect to *obedience to God*. Hence *all* man's necessities are met only in that day which God has sanctified and commanded to be kept.

A judge in Santa Clara, Cal., told me his experience in crossing the Plains with teams in an early day. A large caravan started together. About half the party were in favor of resting upon Sunday. The other half were in so great a hurry that they opposed it and decided to travel every day. So the train divided, one-half resting upon Sunday, and the other traveling every day. The first week or two the Sunday travelers gained a little. After that the second party came up with them and passed them, and kept ahead all the way through. The party which rested every seventh day came through in better health, and with their teams in a much better condition than those who did not.

"In the year 1839, a committee was appointed in the legislature of Pennsylvania, who made a report with regard to the employment of laborers on their canals. In that report they say, in reference to those who had petitioned against the employment of the workmen on the Sabbath, 'They assert, as the result of their experience, that both man and beast can do more work by resting one day in seven than by working on the whole seven.' They then add, 'Your committee feel free to confess that their own experience as business men, farmers, or legislators, corresponds with the assertion.'"

"The experiment was tried in a large flouring establishment. For a number of years they worked the mills seven days in a week. The superintendent was then changed. He ordered the men to stop the works at eleven o'clock on Saturday night, and not to start them till one o'clock on Monday morning, thus allowing a full Sabbath every week. And the same men, during the year, actually ground fifty thousand bushels more than had ever been ground, in a single year, in that establishment before."

"A manufacturing company, which had been accustomed to carry their goods to market with their own teams, kept them employed seven days in a week, as that was the time in which they could go to market and return. But by permitting the teams to rest on the Sabbath, they found that they could drive the same distance in six days that they formerly did in seven, and with the same keeping preserve them in better order."

"Two neighbors in the State of New York,

each with a drove of sheep, started on the same day for a distant market. One started several hours before the other, and traveled uniformly every day. The other rested every Sabbath. Yet he arrived at the market first, with his flock in a better condition than that of the other. In giving an account of it he said that he drove his sheep on Monday about seventeen miles, on Tuesday not over sixteen, and so lessening each day, till on Saturday he drove them only about eleven miles. But on Monday, after resting on the Sabbath, they would travel again seventeen miles, and so on each week. But his neighbor's sheep, which were not allowed to rest on the Sabbath, before they arrived at the market could not travel without injury more than six or eight miles a day."

"A number of men started from Ohio, with droves of cattle for Philadelphia. They had often been before, and had been accustomed to drive on the Sabbath as on other days. One had now changed his views as to the propriety of traveling on that day. On Saturday he inquired for pasture. His associates wondered that so shrewd a man should think of consuming so great a portion of his profits by stopping with such a drove a whole day. He stopped, however, and kept the Sabbath. They, thinking that they could not afford to do so, went on. On Monday he started again. In the course of the week he passed them, arrived first in the market, and sold his cattle to great advantage. So impressed were the others with the benefits of thus keeping the Sabbath that ever afterwards they followed his example."—*The Sabbath Manual,* by Justin Edwards, D. D., pp. 50-52, 56-59.

The above statements show the necessity for a weekly rest-day. They prove nothing in favor of Sunday which these writers call the Sabbath. The same benefits, physically and mentally, would follow from resting upon any stated day of the week. Other considerations determine which day is the Sabbath. But these facts do show that a weekly rest-day is absolutely necessary for physical health and vigor.

Simply resting nights is not sufficient. An occasional holiday is not sufficient. Nothing but a regular rest-day, one day out of every seven, will do. We appeal to the experience of every laboring man who has ever tried both plans, to say if our position is not correct. After a good Sabbath day's rest, with how much more vigor, animation, and even delight, the laboring man can commence another week's work. But alas! how forlorn and hopeless, how pitiable is the case of the man or beast that is compelled to labor on and on without any Sabbath day. It is a violation of a fundamental law which the Creator has stamped upon our nature. These are facts which are equally true in every age of the world, from Adam down, and among all nations, whether Jews or Gentiles, which shows that the Sabbath law meets a natural and universal want of mankind.

Constant thought and mental application in the same direction for seven days in the week is as ruinous to the mind as continued labor is to the body. This has been proved in the cases of students in colleges, lawyers in the prosecution of their business, and of others in like occupations. It is found that a continued disregard of the Sabbath produces a dispirited, listless, and careless habit; and that the same persons can accomplish more mental labor, and make greater progress in their studies, by strictly observing a weekly day of rest, than they can by working seven days in the week. By unbending the mind, or entirely changing the course of one's thoughts and studies, the brain seems to recuperate, so that we can take up our studies at the beginning of another week with a renewed vigor and power of application which those lack who have not had this mental rest. This I know from experience and from careful observation. A proper amount of nightly rest is not enough. Occasional recreation is not sufficient. God's own provision of a weekly day of rest is the only thing that will completely answer the requirements of the case. <u>To whatever a man's mind is steadily applied during six days of the week, that he should entirely drop and lay aside on the seventh day, and turn his thoughts to something else.</u> How admirable, then, is God's provision for a weekly Sabbath day upon which all ordinary pursuits, whether physical or mental, must be laid aside, that that day may be spent in acts of devotion toward God. If this precept of the decalogue is not founded in the nature of man, then there is not one of the ten that is.

Of Sabbath-breaking, Justin Edwards says:—

"It is in opposition to another law; not merely to that which was written on the tables of stone, but to a law written by the finger of God, on the nature of both man and beast. They were not made for seven days' labor in a week, and they cannot endure it without diminishing their strength and shortening their lives.

"The Sabbath institution is not a positive or moral institution merely. It is based upon a *natural* law. And if it is the duty of laboring men not to commit suicide, it is their duty to keep the Sabbath."

Bishop, on Criminal Law, says that "the setting apart by the whole community of one day in seven, wherein the thoughts of men and the physical activities shall be turned into another than their accustomed channels, is a thing pertaining as much to the law of nature as is the intervening of the nights between the days."

"In the year 1832, the British House of Commons appointed a committee to investigate the effects of laboring seven days in a week compared with those of laboring only six and resting one. The committee consisted of about thirty of the most prominent men of Parliament.

"They examined a great number of witnesses, of various professions and employments. Among them was John Richard Farre, M. D., of London, of whom they speak as 'an acute and experienced physician.' The following is his testimony:—

"'I have practiced as a physician between thirty and forty years..... I have had occasion to observe the effect of the observance and non-observance of the seventh day of rest during this time. I have been in the habit during a great many years of considering the *uses* of the Sabbath, and of observing its *abuses*. The abuses are chiefly manifested in labor and dissipation. Its use, medicinally speaking, is that of a day of rest. As a day of rest, I view it as a day of *compensation* for the inadequate restorative power of the body under *continued* labor and excitement.

"'I consider, therefore, that, in the bountiful provision of Providence for the preservation of human life, the Sabbath appointment is not, as it has been sometimes theologically viewed, simply a precept partaking of the nature of a political institution, but that it is to be numbered among the *natural* duties, if the preservation of life be admitted to be a duty, and the premature destruction of it a suicidal act.' This is said simply as a physician, and without reference at all to the theological question.... Researches in *physiology*, by the analogy of the working of Providence in nature, will show that the divine commandment is not to be considered as an arbitrary enactment, but as an appointment *necessary* to man."

"I have found it essential to my own well-being, as a physician, to abridge my labor on the Sabbath to what is actually necessary. I have frequently observed the premature death of medical men from *continued* exertion. In warm climates and in active service this is painfully apparent. I have advised the clergymen also, in lieu of their Sabbath, to rest one day in the week. It forms a continual prescription of mine."

"The working of the mind in one continued train of thought is destructive of life in the most distinguished class of society; and senators themselves stand in need of reform in that particular. I have observed many of them destroyed by neglecting this economy of life. Therefore, to all men, of whatever class, who must necessarily be occupied six days in the week, I would recommend to abstain on the seventh; and in the course of life, by giving to their bodies the repose and to their minds the change of ideas suited to the day, they would assuredly gain by it. In fact, by the increased vigor imparted, more mental work would be accomplished in their lives. A human being is so constituted that he needs a day of rest, both from mental and bodily work."—*Sabbath Manual*, pp. 34–39.

Thomas Sewell, M. D., professor of pathology and the practice of medicine in the Columbian College, Washington, D. C., says: "While I consider it the more important design of the institution of the Sabbath to assist in religious devotion and advance man's spiritual welfare, I have long held the opinion that one of its chief benefits has reference to his *physical* and *intellectual* constitution; affording him, as it does, one day in seven for the renovation of his exhausted energies of body and mind—a proportion of time small enough, according to the results of my observation, for the accomplishment of this object. . . . . I have no hesitation in declaring it as my opinion that, if the Sabbath were universally observed as a day of devotion and of rest from secular occupations, far more work of body and mind would be accomplished, and be better done; more health would be enjoyed, with more of wealth and independence, and we should have far less of crime and poverty and suffering."

Ebenezer Aldin, M. D., of Massachusetts, remarks: "After much reflection, I am satisfied that the Sabbath was made for man, as a physical as well as an intellectual and moral being. . . . . Unnecessary labor on the Sabbath is a *physical sin*, a transgression of a *physical law*, a law to which a penalty is attached—a penalty which cannot be evaded."

Justin Edwards, D. D., bears this testimony: "It is now settled by facts, that the observance of the Sabbath is required by a natural law, and that, were man nothing more than an animal, and were his existence to be confined to this world, it would be for his interest to observe the Sabbath.' —*Sabbath Manual*, p. 60.

A few years since, six hundred and forty-one medical men sent a petition to Parliament upon this subject, in which they say: "Your petitioners from their acquaintance with the laboring classes, and with the laws which regulate the human economy, are convinced that a seventh day of rest, instituted by God, and coeval with the existence of man, is essential to the bodily health and mental vigor of men in every station of life." —*Associated Medical Journal*, June, 1853, p. 554, quoted in *The Sabbath*, by Gilfillan, p. 180.

Such testimonies as these from the most celebrated business men, eminent lawyers, and skillful physicians, could be multiplied to any extent, all testifying to just what we claim, viz., that the Sabbath precept rests upon one of the plainest laws of nature. It is, therefore, moral in its broadest sense.

VI. *Man's moral and spiritual well-being requires just what the Sabbath precept provides, and hence it is moral.*

Here, again, a wide field opens before us; but our space will allow us to explore but a part of it, and that hastily. What are the proper uses of the Sabbath day? Simply the cessation of labor is not all. The day is to be employed in meditating upon God's works, in talking of his greatness and mercies, in studying his word, in going to the house of God for singing, prayer, Sabbath-school, social meeting, hearing the word of God, and like exercises.

Deprive society wholly of this weekly rest-day; abolish your Sabbath-schools, prayer meetings, and regular sermons; let work of all kinds and classes go on seven days in the week, and what would society be? If you want to know, go to heathen lands where they have entirely forgotten the Sabbath, and behold their ignorance, superstition, degradation, and crime. That is just what would follow, in any nation, the abolition of the weekly rest-day. We are social beings, and one of the greatest means of improvement is social intercourse. Take the child that is kept away from Sabbath-schools and Sabbath gatherings, and is kept at work in the same clothes seven days in the week, and he soon becomes degraded, and his moral sensibilities become blunted. There are thousands of such examples as this. On the other hand, it does have a refining and elevating influence upon children and youth to leave their ordinary work once a week, and assemble with others for social and religious purposes. Nothing else can take the place of this. All other means combined scarcely equal in importance the influence of the Sabbath for this purpose.

But take it from a religious point of view, and how inestimable are the benefits and advantages of the Sabbath day. To properly estimate this we must suppose the Sabbath to be entirely laid aside and no fixed rest-day to be regarded by society. What a condition of things we should then behold! We should have no Sabbath-schools, no Bible-classes, no regular days for meetings or divine worship, no day of rest from constant, wearisome toil; but everywhere shops and stores would be open, mills running, farm work going on, and, in short, one continued tide of work, work, work, business and worldliness. The anxiety of the employer to make the most out of his capital, and of the laborer to make the most of his time, crowds out all rest-days. If the poor laborer wishes to rest, his employer will not allow him to do so. If one house closes, the other will take its custom. And so all rush on in hot haste after the world, while God and man's spiritual wants are forgotten!

What could a minister accomplish with such a state of things? How long would the members retain their spirituality? How long would the church survive under such circumstances? Compelled to labor against such disadvantages, it would not have been possible for the church to have accomplished one-hundredth part of what it has— if, indeed, it could have survived at all. By taking advantage of a weekly day of rest, when the people have leisure to come together to hear the word of God, the church has gained its strongest hold upon the people.

In wide contrast with the sad state of things which would result if the no-Sabbath theory were carried out, and the church and the world were entirely deprived of a weekly rest-day, let us suppose for a moment that the Sabbath precept was carefully kept by all the world. What a delightful, what a heavenly sight we should behold! For six days all men are busily and honestly employed in their secular affairs; but now God's holy rest-day comes. All business is suspended; all labor is laid aside; every shop and store is closed; the mills are stopped; the cars and the boats stand still; all toil on the farm is suspended; the beasts are allowed quietly to repose in the barn or in the field; all around the world everything is quiet and still; the children and youth, cleanly and neatly dressed, are wending their way to the Sabbath-school, where they will learn about their Creator, their Saviour, and a pure and holy life. The people gather at the house of God, where solemn prayer and sweet songs of praise are offered to the Lord. The elevating truths of our holy religion are set forth before them. This would be a scene for angels to behold with delight. Heaven would come near to earth, and man would be lifted up into a higher and purer life.

Of the influence of Sabbath observance, an eminent author says:—

"Its calm and heavenly stillness, when, after six days of labor and amusement, the activity, bustle, noise and tumult of worldliness die away, speaks of God. And as the Sabbath sun rises in his glory, and no man goes forth to labor, and all creation seems to listen, there is not an obedient child in the world, who knows the reason of this, and has been taught his duty, who does not feel more than he did before the Omnipresence of Jehovah, and have a more operative conviction that he sees everything, and hears everything, and knows everything, and is of purer eyes than to behold iniquity. Earth becomes like the house of God, and the Sabbath like the gate of Heaven. It seems to raise a ladder like that of Jacob, and to show him angels ascending and descending upon it. He can hardly forbear to say, 'Surely, God is in this place.' For him, in keeping the Sabbath, so to play the fool as to say, even in heart, 'no God,' is next to impossible."—*Sabbath Manual*, pp. 172, 173.

Reader, if the Sabbath day is not a moral institution, then God has never given one to man. It is one of the relics of Eden, a golden link that binds us to the throne of the Creator, and brings Heaven's blessings near to man. May it long remain, with all its hallowed and dear associations.

We grant, says one, that all the above-named evils would follow if there was no regular day for rest and public meeting; but the church or society could agree and fix upon some day for this purpose without a definite appointment by the Lord. Indeed! This admission is the strongest argument in favor of our position; for it admits that the necessity for a Sabbath day is so great that men would appoint one even if God had neglected to do so!! What does this show? Just what I am trying to prove, viz., that God in giving us a Sabbath day simply met a generally felt and acknowledged want of mankind, which grows out of their nature physically, mentally, morally, and spiritually. It shows that the Sabbath rests upon the same basis that all other moral precepts do, viz., the wants of man's nature.

It is a noticeable fact that our opponents who contend that there is no Sabbath day at all, do still keep a weekly rest-day and use it for social and religious purposes. In this we see an illustration of the old proverb, "Nature will out." Why do they do this? The fact is that nature is stronger than their theories, and will assert itself.

Another says, We agree that one-seventh part of time should be set aside as sacred to God; but it makes no difference which day it is, provided all are united upon it, which is the important idea. Here, again, they unwittingly admit all that we claim. They admit that it is a moral duty of man to devote one day in seven to the service of God. Thus they give it a moral basis —just that for which we are contending! Again, they strongly urge the great importance of all uniting to keep the same day. They dwell upon the inconvenience to society, where one keeps one day and another some other day, and so on; how this interferes with business; how each one annoys the other; how it breaks up society, &c. Thus they readily name a long list of evils which follow where men keep different days for the Sabbath.

Do they not see that these very facts overthrow their own position? They maintain that it is no matter which day you keep, provided you keep one day in seven, and that every man has the liberty to choose for himself. Then they turn square about and show how very important it is that all keep the same day! Why, then, do they advocate the very principle which, if carried out, would produce the very division, discord and confusion which they deprecate so much? Did not the Lord have as much wisdom as man? Did he not know that it was important that all should keep the same day? Did he not see that, if he left it to every man to choose what day he would keep, confusion would inevitably follow, as all men would not be likely to choose the same day? Is God so unwise as to leave his laws in this slack manner? Is this not charging God with folly? What is gained to God or man by leaving every man thus to choose what day he will keep? The only way that union could be secured in observing the Sabbath, would be for the Lord himself to designate the definite day which all must keep. Then all would keep the same day, and all confusion would be avoided. We say, then, that reason and the nature of things teach us that if God should give man a Sabbath day at all, it should be a definite day, selected and appointed by God himself. That this is just what God has done in the Sabbath precept we will now show.

"Remember the Sabbath day, to keep it holy. Six days shalt thou labor, and do all thy work; but the seventh day is the Sabbath of the Lord thy God; in it thou shalt not do any work, thou, nor thy son, nor thy daughter, thy man-servant, nor thy maid-servant, nor thy cattle, nor thy stranger that is within thy gates; for in six days the Lord made heaven and earth, the sea, and all that in them is, and rested the seventh day; wherefore the Lord blessed the Sabbath day, and hallowed it." Ex. 20: 8–11.

Notice this language carefully, and see if it does not designate a definite, particular day, not merely one day in seven, or simply one-seventh part of our time. The Lord says, "Remember the Sabbath day." What are we to remember? Not the *Sabbath*, but the Sabbath *day*, or rather, the day of the Sabbath. The *day*, then, is the important thing which we are to remember. The Lord does not say that we shall remember *a* Sabbath day, *some* Sabbath day, *any* Sabbath day, one day out of seven, or one-seventh part of our time. No such indefinite language is used; but it is just as definite as language can make it. "Remember *the* Sabbath day." The definite article *the* is used. If we wish to point out a definite, particular man, we say *the* man. Otherwise, we say *a* man. So, here, the Lord says *the* day, the Sabbath day. But which day is that? He makes it still more definite. "Six days shalt thou labor, and do all thy work; but the seventh day," &c. "Well," says one, "that is just what we do. We work six days and rest on the seventh, and this is all that the commandment requires; viz., that we should rest one day after six days of work, no matter where we begin to count."

But look a little farther. The Lord does not leave it in that way. Which seventh day we shall rest upon is pointed out in the most definite manner. "But the seventh day is the Sabbath of the Lord thy God; in it thou shalt not do any work," &c. Here, again, we notice the Lord does not say *a* seventh day, nor one day in seven, nor one-seventh part of time, nor is any such indefinite expression used. It is *the* seventh day.

But now comes the clincher, which settles beyond all doubt just which seventh day we must rest upon. "But the seventh day is the Sabbath of the Lord thy God; in it," &c. Which seventh day are we to keep? It is that one which is the *Sabbath day,* or *rest-day, of the Lord.* Sabbath signifies rest. Sabbath day, rest-day. The Sabbath day of the Lord, the rest-day of the Lord, or the day upon which the Lord rested. Now which day is this? Let the same commandment tell us. "For in six days the Lord made heaven and earth, the sea, and all that in them is, and rested the seventh day; wherefore the Lord blessed the Sabbath day, and hallowed it."

The Lord worked upon each of the first six days of the week. He did not rest upon any of these days. Hence neither of them is his rest, or Sabbath, day. Then he did rest upon the seventh day, the last day of the week. Nor was this simply one-seventh part of time, and no day in particular. It was a definite day, the last day of the week, and no other. When the Lord had rested upon the seventh day, that day thus became distinguished above all other days as the rest-day, or Sabbath day, of the Lord, as Sabbath signifies rest.

To illustrate: Washington was born on the 22d of February. That day thus became distinguished as Washington's birthday. The day of the month, and of the year upon which he was born, and no other day, was, is, and always must be, Washington's birthday. Could he change his birthday from the day upon which he was born to one upon which he was not born? Certainly not. Just so the Lord's rest-day must come upon the very day of the week upon which he rested. The commandment requires us to keep, not our rest-day, nor the Jews' rest-day, nor the Christian's rest-day, but to keep the *Lord's* rest-day. Which day is that? Every honest man must answer that it is the day upon which God rested.

Notice now how plainly the Lord has stated this. "Six days shalt thou labor, and do all thy work; but the seventh day is the Sabbath of the Lord thy God; in it thou shalt not do any work." The seventh day, then, upon which we must rest, must be the one upon which God rested; else it would not be the Lord's rest-day. The commandment, therefore, was given to guard God's rest-day and not some other day which any man's fancy might choose. Did God bless and hallow a day? Yes. Which was it? His own rest-day, for so the commandment says. Are there other days upon which God did not rest? Certainly. Has the Lord sanctified any of these? No, indeed. Thus we might go on to show in the plainest manner that the language of the fourth commandment in the most distinct and definite manner designates as the Sabbath day, not simply one day in seven, but the very day upon which the Creator himself rested, the seventh and last day of the week. This view of the case is consistent. It is eminently reasonable that God should require men to reverence his own hallowed rest-day; and farther, as we have already shown, in requiring man to keep a rest-day, it is unreasonable to believe that God should leave it to every man to select which day he will keep, as no benefit would accrue to any one by such an arrangement; but great confusion and inconvenience must of necessity be brought upon all by such a course. God could easily designate a definite day, which all must keep; and thus harmony would be secured. And this is just what the Lord has done in the fourth commandment.

VII. *The fact that God himself has associated the Sabbath with the moral precepts affords conclusive proof that it is a moral institution.*

Fallen man has one document which came directly from the living God himself, and that is the ten commandments. God came down personally upon Mount Sinai amidst thunderings and lightnings and most terrible majesty, and there, in the hearing of the whole nation, he spoke from Heaven, with his own voice, his moral law of ten commandments.

Webster, in defining the moral law, says that it is "summarily contained in the ten commandments." When God spoke this law, his voice shook the earth. Heb. 12:26. With his own divine finger he then engraved it in imperishable stone; Ex. 31:18; here again indicating that this law was as imperishable and as enduring as the solid rock. It was then deposited in the ark, under the shekinah in the holy of holies. No other part of the Bible, no other law of God, was ever given in such a solemn manner. Why was this? This question our opponents have never been able to answer. Nine of these ten commandments are universally acknowledged to be moral in their nature, and of perpetual and universal application, applying through all ages, and to all nations. Look at them. 1. You shall have no other gods. 2. You shall not make and worship an image. 3. You shall not profane God's name. 5. Honor your parents. 6. Do not kill. 7. Do not commit adultery. 8. Do not steal. 9. Do not bear false witness. 10. Do not covet.

Reader, are not these commandments all moral, and as enduring as truth itself? There is not a shadowy or ceremonial precept in the whole ten, except it be the Sabbath. Now, we ask the reader, If the Sabbath was, unlike the other nine precepts, a mere ceremonial institution, why did

God place it in the moral law? Why did he not put it where it belonged, with those precepts which are confessedly only types and shadows? Shall we impugn God's wisdom to sustain our theories? Would God mar an otherwise perfect moral law? God's own action gives the lie to that baseless theory. It is a true saying that a man is known by the company he keeps. Now look at the Sabbath. God, who knew its character, has placed it in the midst of a strictly moral neighborhood. It has three perfectly moral neighbors on one side, and six on the other. We claim that this important fact shows that the all-wise God has put his stamp upon the Sabbath as a moral institution. What God has joined together let no man put asunder.

VIII. *The Sabbath precept guards the right of property the same as the eighth commandment does; and hence, like that, is moral.*

All admit that the eighth commandment, "Thou shalt not steal," is a moral commandment. Why? Because it guards the right of property. You shall not take and appropriate to your own use that which belongs to another. The Creator, who is the author of everything, has divided time into weeks of seven days each. All these days were the Lord's; but he, in his benevolence and goodness, has given six of them to man to be properly used in his own necessary business, but the seventh day, God's rest-day, he has reserved to himself. The fourth precept is given to guard this Sabbath day. It forbids our appropriating to our own use that which belongs to another, viz., to God. The right of property, then, is recognized in this commandment the same as in the eighth commandment; and, hence, if one is moral the other is also for the same reason.

To illustrate: A wealthy man has seven apple trees, all bearing fruit. He has a poor neighbor living near him. He takes him into the orchard and tells him to freely use of the fruit of the first six trees; but the seventh one he forbids him to touch, as that he has reserved for a special purpose to himself. This would be a very generous act on the part of the rich man. Now how ungrateful and wicked it would be on the part of the poor man to use not only the fruit from the six trees, but to take that of the seventh also. It would be a grossly immoral act.

Just so God has given us six days which we can freely use in an honorable manner; but the seventh day belongs to God. Thus the Lord says by the mouth of Isaiah: "If thou turn away thy foot from the Sabbath, from doing thy pleasure on *my* holy day," &c. Chap. 58:13. Again, the Lord says, "Verily *my* Sabbaths ye shall keep." Ex. 31:13. And so the fourth commandment says, "The seventh day is the Sabbath of the Lord thy God." Ex. 20:10. It is not our day, our time, nor our property. It belongs to God.

And the fourth commandment is given to

guard the Lord's right to this day. Another prophet exclaims, "Will a man rob God? But ye say, Wherein have we robbed thee? In tithes and offerings. Ye are cursed with a curse; for ye have robbed me, even this whole nation." Mal. 3:8, 9. God had reserved to himself one-tenth of all their increase. This belonged to him. Thus he says, "And all the tithe of the land, whether of the seed of the land, or of the fruit of the tree, is the Lord's; it is holy unto the Lord." Lev. 27:30. But the people had taken these tithes which belonged to the Lord and had used them for their own benefit. In doing this they had "robbed God." Then a man can rob the Lord.

If this was true in the above case, with how much greater force can it be said that a man robs God who every week takes God's holy day and appropriates it to his own worldly purposes! Verily, he is guilty of stealing. A little reflection will show that the same motive which leads a man to steal from his neighbor, also leads him to break the Sabbath. He covets his neighbor's property, that he may use it for his own selfish purposes; so he takes it without his consent. So a man covets God's holy day, that he may use it in his own worldly business or pleasure; hence he proceeds to appropriate that sacred time to his own purposes. A man who knowingly appropriates God's Sabbath to his own use is robbing God, and thus violating the very highest principle of morality. If it is wrong to rob our neighbor who is our equal, how much more wicked is it to rob God our Creator? The same moral principle, then, is involved in the Sabbath precept that is in the precept against theft; and therefore it is moral for the same reason.

IX. *Marriage is a moral institution. The Sabbatic institution being made at the same time, by the same authority, for the same persons, and in a similar manner, is also moral for the same reason.*

Notice the origin of the marriage institution. 1. Adam was created; but there was no marriage institution, nor any moral obligation upon Adam touching it. 2. Eve was made; but still there was no marriage institution. 3. Eve was given to Adam to be his wife. Now marriage obligation first existed. It was made by the direct and positive appointment of God. So of the Sabbath. 1. God created the heavens and the earth; but there was no Sabbath yet. 2. God rested the seventh day; still there was no institution of the Sabbath. 3. God blessed and sanctified (set apart to a holy use) the rest-day, and then Sabbath obligation existed.

To deny the morality of the Sabbatic institution because it rests upon the appointment of God, is to deny the morality of the marriage institution; for it rests upon the same authority. If one is moral, the other is also. Indeed, there is a striking similarity in the Bible record touching these two institutions. 1. God himself instituted marriage; so he did the Sabbath. 2. Marriage was instituted before the fall; so was the Sabbath. 3. Paul says: "The woman [was made] for the man;" 1 Cor. 11:9; and Jesus says: "The Sabbath was made for man." Mark 2:27. 4. The apostle says: "Marriage is honorable;" Heb. 13:4; and the Lord exhorts all to call the Sabbath "honorable." Isa. 58:13. These two are the only institutions which the Lord has ever called honorable, thus giving them a pre-eminence. 5. The husband is called the "lord" of the wife; 1 Pet. 3:6; and so the Son of man is called the "Lord" of the Sabbath. Mark 2:28. As the husband loves and cherishes the wife, so the Lord loves and protects his Sabbath. 6. As God has put in the moral law a precept guarding the sacredness of the marriage institution, so he has put in the same law a commandment guarding the sacredness of the Sabbatic institution.

The Jews, having perverted both these institutions, questioned Christ concerning the nature of each of them. His answer in each case was similar. In relation to marriage, his answer, in substance, was this: In the beginning God made *one* man and *one* woman, designing that they *two* should be one flesh. The marriage institution, therefore, was designed to unite but *two* persons, and this union should be *sacred, permanent,* and for man's good. Matt. 19:3–9. Touching the Sabbath, his argument was this: God made the Sabbath. Thus he goes right back to

Eden, the origin of the Sabbath; for that was when the Sabbath was made. Then he says it was made *for* man. Being made for man before he fell, it must be a merciful institution, of which fact the Jews had lost sight. Thus Jesus traces both institutions back to their origin in Eden. Both rest upon a similar basis, and both are equally moral.

X. *The Sabbath precept, like all moral precepts, applies equally well to all nations, in all countries, and at all times.*

All moral laws are of universal application. They are not restricted to one nation or to one country, nor do they change with circumstances; but, on the other hand, merely ceremonial precepts are, from their very nature, restricted in their application to certain persons, times, and places. Here, again, we find evidence of the morality of the Sabbath. As we have shown already, God instituted the Sabbath at creation in Eden before the fall. From this fact several important conclusions necessarily follow.

1. It is not a type. Types were given after the fall to shadow forth redemption; but the Sabbath points back to creation, not forward to redemption. See Ex. 20:11.

2. The fact that the Sabbath was given in the Edenic state indicates that it was designed to be a perpetual institution. Hence we read that when the curse shall be removed from this old earth, and the new-earth state shall be brought

in, then the Sabbath will still be observed, and that forever. Isa. 66:22, 23.

3. It is not a Jewish Sabbath. The simple fact that it was given at creation, twenty-three hundred years before such a distinction existed, proves this.

A Jew is a descendant of Judah, one of the twelve tribes. But Judah himself was not born till nearly twenty-three hundred years after creation. Hence it is absurd to call it a Jewish institution. It is never so called in the Bible, but it is ever designated as God's holy Sabbath.

The Sabbath was given to Adam, who was the representative head of the whole human race, the father of all men and all nations. Acts 17:26. In giving it to him, God thereby gave it to man as a race; hence Christ says truly, "The Sabbath was made for man." Mark 2:27. He does not say it was made for the Jew man, nor for the Gentile man, nor for the Christian man; nor does he limit it in any manner; but he puts it on the broad basis that it was made for man. It is a rule in grammar that a noun unlimited by an adjective is to be taken in its broadest sense, as, "Man is mortal," meaning all men, the race. So in this case; Christ does not limit it to one class of men, but says that it was made for "man," that is, the race.

In this language, he points us back to the time when the Sabbath was made, and says that it was made for man. When was the Sabbath made? It was made at creation. God rested on the seventh day, blessed it, and sanctified it. This is how and when it was made. For whom was it made? Christ's language is definite. It "was made for man." <u>Being given to Adam, the father of the Gentiles as well as of the Jews, it was thus given to all nations</u>; for Paul says that God "hath made of one blood all nations of men for to dwell on all the face of the earth." Acts 17:26.

A careful examination of the commandment will show that it is equally applicable to all nations in all ages. Read it carefully. "Remember the Sabbath day, to keep it holy." Cannot Gentiles do that as well as the Jews? Can we not do it as well in America as in Asia?

"Six days shalt thou labor, and do all thy work." Is not that enough for any man to work in any country, or in any nation? Can the Gentiles endure to work more days than the Jews? Have we not already shown that all men need a day of rest after six days of labor?

"But the seventh day is the Sabbath of the Lord thy God." Is not the seventh day God's rest-day now as truly as it was then? Does it not remain a fact now that God did rest upon the seventh day? and as long as this continues to be a fact, will it not be true that the seventh day is God's rest-day? Certainly.

"In it thou shalt not do any work." We need a day of rest and worship now as much as then, the Gentiles as much as the Jews.

"Thou, nor thy son, nor thy daughter, thy

man-servant, nor thy maid-servant, nor thy cattle, nor thy stranger that is within thy gates." Do not all these relations exist now among all nations! Do they not all have sons and daughters, servants and cattle? And do not all these need the rest of the Sabbath? Certainly.

"For in six days the Lord made heaven, and earth, the sea, and all that in them is." Is it not just as true now as it was then that God created all things in six days and rested the seventh day? Does not this remain a fact now?

"Wherefore [that is, for this reason] the Lord blessed the Sabbath day, and hallowed it." Why did the Lord bless the Sabbath day and hallow it? Because that in it he had rested from all his work.

As we have shown, the Lord set apart the seventh day as a memorial of creation. Who should observe that memorial? All who are interested in creation. Verily, are not the Gentiles as much interested in the work of creation as the Jews ever were? As Paul significantly asks, "Is he the God of the Jews only? is he not also of the Gentiles? Yes, of the Gentiles also." Rom. 3: 29. Was it not, then, true that God created the Gentiles as well as the Jews; and did not the Gentiles inhabit the earth which he there created? Are they not constantly enjoying the blessings which he there made for man? Certainly. Then why should they not be as much interested to commemorate this great work as were the Jews?

In short, there is not a single idea in the fourth commandment but applies equally well to all nations, in all countries, and at all times. Did the Jews need a day of rest? So do the Gentiles. Did the Jews need a day for religious worship? So do the Gentiles. The Jews kept the seventh day to commemorate creation; so should the Gentiles.

XI. *The Sabbath is the seal to God's moral law, without which, that law would be of no authority.*

Every government has its seal, and every office its seal. It has been found very important that this should be so. This seal is always attached to every law, edict, or document, put forth by the government or the officers of the government, and they would be of no authority without it. Its object is to point out the author of the document—what his office is, and how far his jurisdiction extends. This is necessary in order that the subjects of any power may not be imposed upon by an impostor. This seal is a sign of the authority of the one issuing such law, edict, or official document.

To illustrate: John Brown is elected justice of the peace for a certain township. It becomes necessary for him to issue a warrant for the arrest of Mr. Jones. He writes it in due form; but, being a novice in the business, he simply signs his name John Brown. The sheriff proceeds to arrest Mr. Jones. But Jones, being a sharp man and wishing to gain time, demands the officer's authority for arresting him. The sheriff shows him the warrant. "John Brown," says Jones, "who is John Brown? There are many John Browns in this world. I don't run at the call of every John Brown." What could the sheriff do? His warrant is worthless. It has no authority. Why? Because it has no evidence of authority. But now let Brown just add the title of his office to that warrant, then Mr. Jones will have to respect it. The signature now stands, "John Brown, Justice of the Peace, for such a township." This tells which Brown it is, what his office is, and how far his authority extends.

Take it in a higher office. Every lawful document issued by our President must have the sign of his office attached. Simply signing his name, "U. S. Grant," would give it no authority. To this he must add, "President of the United States." "U. S. Grant" tells his name; "President" tells his office; "of the United States," tells how far his authority extends. This, then, is the nature and object of a seal.

Now if a seal is so important in human laws, how much more so in the divine law? Has the living God no seal? Reason itself would teach us that he has; but the Bible settles this beyond dispute. "And I saw another angel ascending from the east, having *the seal of the living God.*" Rev. 7:2. Then the living God has a seal, and this seal is in his law; for thus we read: "Bind up the testimony, *seal the law* among my disciples." Isa. 8:16.

As we have shown, no law is of any authority unless it contains the seal of the lawgiver; and this seal must be in the handwriting of the one issuing such law. If, therefore, the living God has ever given a law in his own handwriting, then that law will contain his seal. The moral law, the ten commandments, was given by God and written with his finger. "And the Lord said unto Moses, Come up to me into the mount, and be there; and I will give thee tables of stone, and a law, and commandments which I have written; that thou mayest teach them." Ex. 24:12. "And he gave unto Moses, when he had made an end of communing with him upon Mount Sinai, two tables of testimony, tables of stone, written with the finger of God." Ex. 31:18.

Now let us examine this law, and see if we can find God's seal in it. A seal, remember, is to point out the author of the law, what his office is, and how far his jurisdiction extends. To bring out the thought clearly, we will suppose that a missionary is sent to convert the heathen who have never heard of the true God, but are worshipers of the sun. Of course, his first effort must be to convince them that they are not worshiping the true God, and hence are sinners. He learns from Paul that "by the law is the knowledge of sin;" Rom. 3:20; and that without the law a man would not know sin. Rom. 7:7; James 2:9; Rom. 4:15; 5:13. Obtaining a congregation of these heathen, he reads them the first commandment.

"Thou shalt have no other gods before me." "Me," says one, "whom does he mean by *me*? Does he mean himself?" "Oh, no," says another, "he means our god, the sun. We don't have any other gods before him." What could the missionary do? This commandment does not show who the true God is. It does not tell who gave this law, nor what his authority is. But the missionary knows that the law must point out the true God, so he reads the second commandment.

"Thou shalt not make unto thee any graven image, or any likeness of anything that is in heaven above, or that is in the earth beneath, or that is in the water under the earth; thou shalt not bow down thyself to them, nor serve them; for I the Lord thy God am a jealous God, visiting the iniquity of the fathers upon the children unto the third and fourth generation of them that hate me; and showing mercy unto thousands of them that love me and keep my commandments." They all exclaim, "Oh, we never make any images to our god, the sun. Of course, we will love him; for he promises to show mercy to those who do." Here the missionary finds himself balked again. Still he is confident that the law will point out the true

God, who alone must be worshiped. He reads the next commandment.

"Thou shalt not take the name of the Lord thy God in vain; for the Lord will not hold him guiltless that taketh his name in vain." Once more they reply, "No, indeed, we never speak the name of our god, the sun, but with the greatest reverence." Here he is stranded again. He would read the fourth commandment, but he thinks that it never was of much account, and has been abolished any way, so he reads the fifth.

"Honor thy father and thy mother; that thy days may be long upon the land which the Lord thy God giveth thee." "There," say they, "our god, the sun, will give us long life if we honor our parents." The missionary now runs over the other five precepts, but does not find the name of God in them at all, nor anything which tells who is the author of this law, nor anything by which he can convince these heathen that they are not worshiping the true God. As his last hope, he now turns and reads the only remaining commandment, the Sabbath precept.

"Remember the Sabbath day, to keep it holy. Six days shalt thou labor, and do all thy work; but the seventh day is the Sabbath of the Lord thy God; in it thou shalt not do any work, thou, nor thy son, nor thy daughter, thy man-servant, nor thy maid-servant, nor thy cattle, nor thy stranger that is within thy gates; for in six days the Lord made heaven and earth, the sea, and all that in them is, and rested the seventh day;

wherefore the Lord blessed the Sabbath day and hallowed it." Ah! here he has the very thing for which he has been so long looking. Who is the author of this law? It is the one who made heaven and earth, and all things in them. He is the one who made the sun which these heathen are worshiping. Hence they are idolaters, not worshiping the God who gave this law.

Thus it will be seen that this commandment is the one, and the only one of the whole law, which does point out the true God and author of the law. The law was divided into two parts and written upon two tables of stone—the first four commandments relating to man's duty to God, his Creator, upon the first table; and the last six precepts, relating to our duty to our neighbor, upon the second table. At the bottom of the first table God signed his name and put his seal to it. After giving the first four commandments, the Lord then gives the authority by which he commands them to do these things. Thus: "For in six days the LORD [here he writes his name —the LORD] made [this gives his office—MAKER of] heaven and earth, the sea, and all that in them is; and rested the seventh day [this shows how far his authority extends—through heaven and earth. The Lord did thus formally sign and seal his own divine law. Then he adds], wherefore the Lord blessed the Sabbath day, and hallowed it."

Thus plainly is it shown that the Sabbath precept does contain the seal to God's law, without which that law would be of no authority whatever. There is nothing else in the whole law which shows by whom or by what authority it was given. This fact alone elevates the Sabbath precept to the highest moral importance. It shows that all the other precepts of the moral law depend for their authority upon the fact set forth in the fourth commandment and commemorated by the seventh-day Sabbath. The Lord says to me, Thou shalt not kill. Thou shalt not steal, &c. What gave him the right thus to command me? Answer. The very fact that he is my Creator and the Maker of all the earth. So important a fact as this upon which rests God's authority as a lawgiver should be sacredly guarded and the knowledge of it carefully preserved among men.

As we have abundantly shown, this was the very object for which the Sabbath was given. God made the earth in six days and rested on the seventh. Did God rest because he was tired? No, indeed, for he neither fainteth nor is weary (Isa. 40:28); but evidently he did it to lay the foundation of an institution for man by which he could commemorate God's great work of creation. At the close of six days' labor as we celebrate God's rest-day, it becomes a weekly reminder of the great work of creation and our obligation to our Maker. Creative power is the distinguishing attribute of the living God, and to this the Lord always appeals as the evidence of his existence, his power, and his authority, and as that which distinguishes him from all false gods.

Notice how prominent this fact is always made in the Bible. It is the very first thing mentioned in the word of God. Gen. 1:1. "In the beginning God created the heaven and the earth." David says, "For all the gods of the people are idols; but the Lord made the heavens." 1 Chron. 16:26. Nehemiah thus exalts him: "Thou, even thou, art Lord alone; thou hast made heaven, the heaven of heavens, with all their host, the earth, and all things that are therein, the seas, and all that is therein, and thou preservest them all." Neh. 9:6. The psalmist thus gives the reason why all should fear God: "Let all the earth [Gentiles as well as Jews] fear the Lord; let all the inhabitants of the world stand in awe of him. [Why?] For he spake, and it was done; he commanded, and it stood fast." Ps. 33:8, 9. "Serve the Lord with gladness; come before his presence with singing. Know ye that the Lord he is God; it is he that made us, and not we ourselves. Ps. 100:2, 3. When David would designate what God he relies upon he says, "My help cometh from the Lord, which made heaven and earth." Ps. 121:2. Again he says, "Happy is he that hath the God of Jacob for his help, whose hope is in the Lord his God; which made heaven, and earth, the sea, and all that therein is." Ps. 146:5, 6.

Here are set forth, as the mark of the true God,

the very facts named in the fourth commandment as the basis of the Sabbath. See Ex. 30:11. Hezekiah in the time of his great distress cried to God thus: "O Lord God of Israel, which dwellest between the cherubim, thou art the God, even thou alone, of all the kingdoms of the earth; thou hast made heaven and earth. . . . Of a truth, Lord, the kings of Assyria have destroyed the nations and their lands, and have cast their gods into the fire; for they were no gods, but the work of men's hands, wood and stone." 2 Kings 19:15-18. Thus Hezekiah distinguishes the true God from the false gods by the fact that he created heaven and earth. Jeremiah uses the same arguments against the heathen gods. "But the Lord is the true God, he is the living God, and an everlasting King; at his wrath the earth shall tremble, and the nations shall not be able to abide his indignation. Thus shall ye say unto them, The gods that have not made the heavens and the earth, even they shall perish from the earth, and from under these heavens. He hath made the earth by his power, he hath established the world by his wisdom, and hath stretched out the heavens by his discretion." Jer. 10:10-12.

The fact that God made heaven and earth is that to which the Lord always appeals as the proof of his existence and authority. In the Bible great prominence is everywhere given to this fact. No wonder that God has set apart one day in the week to celebrate and commemorate this great event, upon the proof of which his authority as lawgiver rests. Once the Lord commanded Jeremiah to send a message to the heathen kings of Moab, Edom, Zidon, &c. But they did not know the Lord. How should their servants describe the God who sent the message? The Lord told him to introduce him thus: "Thus shall ye say unto your masters: I have made the earth, the man and the beast that are upon the ground, by my great power," &c. Jer. 27:4, 5. When Jonah wished to tell the heathen what God he served, he said, "I fear the Lord, the God of Heaven, which hath made the sea and the dry land." Jonah 1:9.

Turning to the New Testament, we find the Christian writers using the same facts in describing the living God. Thus at Lystra, when the heathen were about to worship Paul and Barnabas, Paul cried out, "Sirs, why do ye these things? We also are men of like passions with you, and preach unto you that ye should turn from these vanities unto the living God, which made heaven, and earth, and the sea, and all things that are therein." Acts 14:15. So again, when Paul wished to introduce to the Athenians the true God, he says, "As I passed by, and beheld your devotions, I found an altar with this inscription, TO THE UNKNOWN GOD. Whom therefore ye ignorantly worship, him declare I unto you. God that made the world and all things therein, seeing that he is Lord of Heaven and earth, dwelleth not in temples made with hands." Acts 17:23, 24. See also Ps. 89:11, 12; 96:5;

124:8; 148:5, 6; Isa. 40:18-28; 42:5; 44:24; 45:12, 18; 51:13; Jer. 51:15; Rev. 4:11; 10:6; 14:7. Finally Paul says, "For the invisible things of Him from the creation of the world are clearly seen, being understood by the things that are made, even his eternal power and Godhead; so that they are without excuse." Rom. 1:20. Thus we always find all the inspired writers of both the Old and the New Testament appealing to the facts of the creation in proof of the existence and authority of God; the proof and memory of which facts the Sabbath was given to perpetuate among men. The Lord expressly says that he gave his people his holy Sabbath, that hereby they might know that they were worshiping the true God. Thus he says: "Verily my Sabbaths ye shall keep; for it is a sign between me and you throughout your generations, that ye may know that I am the Lord that doth sanctify you." Ex. 31:13. "And hallow my Sabbaths; and they shall be a sign between me and you, that ye may know that I am the Lord your God." Eze. 20:20. For what did the Lord give them the Sabbath? For a sign, by which they might know the Lord. So, then, there is that in the Sabbath commandment which does point out the true God, the Creator of heaven and earth, the author of the moral law.

This being true, the moral importance of the careful preservation of the Sabbath among men cannot be overestimated. To simply secure to man a day of rest and worship is but a small part of the object for which the Sabbath was instituted. No, the great design of the Sabbath is that it should be a memorial of creation, a sign of the true God, and a seal to his immutable law. In this light we can see why the all-wise God, who never makes a mistake, placed the Sabbath in the moral law. It was because it serves the highest of all moral purposes, viz., to point out the true God, the Author of the law. None can fail to see that if we remove the Sabbath precept from the ten commandments, there is nothing left in the law to tell who the lawgiver is, what his authority is, or how far it extends. It would leave the law incomplete and without any authority whatever. This shows that the Sabbath precept is a necessary part of, and a seal to, the moral law, and hence is in the highest sense a moral commandment.

XII. *The seventh-day Sabbath differed from all other holy days in many important points.*

1. It had for its basis God's own act of creation. Gen. 2:1-3. God worked six days and rested the seventh. This, as we have shown, was the basis of the seventh-day Sabbath. This was not true of any other holy day ever given to man.

2. The seventh-day Sabbath was the rest-day of God himself. Ex. 20:11. This was not true of any other holy day. Why do we keep the seventh day? Because the Creator himself rested

upon it. Is this true of any other day? No, indeed. This fact alone puts an infinite difference between God's holy rest-day and all other rest-days.

3. The seventh-day Sabbath was commanded by God's own voice, speaking from Heaven. Neh. 9:13, 14. Here is another fact which is not true of any other day.

4. It was twice written by the finger of the living God. Ex. 24:12; Deut. 10:1-5. No other day was ever thus given.

5. It was engraven on tables of stone. This probably was to indicate its enduring and unchangeable nature. The law relating to other holy days was written by men upon parchment, indicating that, like the material upon which it was written, they were soon to pass away—not so of God's rest-day.

6. The seventh-day Sabbath was placed in the moral law. Ex. 20:1-17. No others were. This is a stubborn fact which our opponents can never account for. If the Sabbath was a mere typical, shadowy, or ceremonial institution, as were the festival days of the Jews, why did God himself put it in the moral law, and thus associate it with moral precepts? Why did he not place it with the other Jewish holy days if it was like them? Did God make a mistake and place it where it did not belong? Our opponents, with their view of the Sabbath, certainly never would have put it where God did, in the moral law. Here God has marked an important

difference between the Sabbath and all other sacred days.

7. This law was placed in the ark, in the most holy place. Deut. 10:1-5; 1 Kings 8:9 The law regulating the festival days was not thus honored, but was written in a book and placed by the side of the ark. Deut. 31:24-26.

8. All other holy days grew out of man's actions as a sinner, and they would never have existed but for sin. Here we have a marked contrast which we wish the reader to distinctly notice. The Sabbath grew out of the action of a holy and infinite God, but all festival days originated in some action of man himself. See a complete list of these days in Lev. 23.

9. All other holy days originated this side of the fall, after types and shadows were introduced. This marks them as shadowy and typical. But the Sabbath, as we have shown, was given in Eden before types were instituted.

10. The Gentiles could keep the Sabbath without being circumcised; Ex. 20:10,11; Rom. 2:24-27; but in order to keep the other festivals they must be circumcised. Ex. 12:48.

11. The people had to go up to Jerusalem to keep the other holy days; Ex. 23:14-17; but they kept the Sabbath in all parts of the country wherever they were.

12. The seventh-day Sabbath was weekly, but all other holy days were yearly.

So many and so marked differences between God's holy Sabbath and all other holy days show that they are of very different natures—the first was unchangeable, perpetual, and for all people; but the second was only ceremonial, temporal, and for one nation.

OBJECTIONS CONSIDERED.

We will now consider the objections which are urged to show that the Sabbath is not a moral precept. We are willing to give them their full weight, confident that they can all be fairly answered.

OBJ. I. *All moral principles are discoverable by the light of nature; but the keeping of the seventh day holy is not discoverable by the light of nature or reason without a direct revelation from God; therefore, it is not moral.*

The answer to this objection is two-fold. First, it assumes what is not true in the case of the other moral commandments; and, secondly, it denies what is true concerning the *principle* of Sabbatic observance.

1. The first commandment says, "Thou shalt have no other gods before me." The great principle here taught is that men shall worship God. This principle has been universally recognized by all nations as we see in the fact that all do have some god or gods which they worship. Phrenology shows that man is organized to worship. He has the organ of veneration, the only legitimate use of which is to worship the Supreme Being. Hence, all nations have mani-

fested the same inclination to worship some god. Thus far all is easy and plain. But the commandment demands more than this. It requires that men shall worship the *true* God and *no other*. Now, have men by *reason* and the *light of nature* alone been able to find the true God without a revelation? No, indeed. The history of the world shows just the opposite. Only a few of the human race have ever known the true God, and these only by a direct revelation as given in the Bible. The language of Paul is directly to the point. "For after that in the wisdom of God the *world by wisdom knew not God*, it pleased God by the foolishness of preaching to save them that believe." 1 Cor. 1 : 21. Of the heathen, he says: "Professing themselves to be wise, they became fools, and changed the glory of the uncorruptible God into an image made like to corruptible man, and to birds, and four-footed beasts, and creeping things." Rom. 1 : 22, 23. This is what men have done who had only the light of nature. None of them have ever been able to find the true God.

Facts bear out this statement to the letter. The learned Dr. Horne says, "In fact, without such revelation, the history of past ages has shown that mere reason *cannot* attain to a *certain* knowledge of the will or law of God." "While some philosophers asserted the being of a God, others openly denied it; others, again, embraced, or pretended to embrace, the notion of a multiplicity of gods." Thus, in Tartary, the

Philippine Islands, and among the savage nations of Africa, the objects of worship are the sun, moon, and stars, the four elements, and serpents; at Tonquin, the several quarters of the earth; in Guinea, birds, fishes, and even mountains; and almost everywhere, evil spirits; together with idolatrous worship, sorcery, divination, and magic, almost universally prevail. . . . . . In Hindoostan, indeed, the polytheism is of the grossest kind, not fewer than *three hundred and thirty millions of deities* claiming the adoration of their worshipers. *Horne's Introduction*, vol. i, pp. 16, 21.

The truth, then, is just this: Quite generally all men have felt that they should worship *some* god; but in selecting *which* it should be, the light of nature has failed them entirely, so that upon this point there has been the greatest confusion, and most have failed to find the true God. None have done it without a revelation.

Just the same thing exactly is true of the Sabbath. That precept is based upon the principle that men should devote a portion of their time as holy to the service of God. As we have proved, man's physical and mental organization shows that he ought to have a regular rest-day. All nations, with scarcely an exception, have recognized this principle by setting apart certain days as holy to the Deity. By tradition from creation most of these have selected a seventh day, while all have had some holy days, more or less, during the year. Says a recent author,

"Traces of sacred days of some sort, though varying in frequency in different countries, may be discovered in many pagan nations, the exceptions being limited to certain tribes sunk, like the aborigines of New Holland, to a very low point in the social scale.

"The Phœnicians, according to Porphyry, 'consecrated the seventh day as holy.' Before Mahommed's time, the Saracens kept their Sabbath on Friday, and from them he and his followers adopted the custom. It is stated by Purchas, that the natives of Pegu had a weekly day upon which they assembled to receive instruction from a class of men appointed for that purpose. The Pagan Slavonians held a weekly festival. In the greater part of Guinea, a seventh day —Tuesday—is set apart to religious worship. . . . . . The Burman feasts are held at the full and change of the moon. According to another authority, the quarters are also observed as festivals. A sacrifice was celebrated by the Mexicans every month. . . . . . The inhabitants of Madagascar and of Senegambia, on the other hand, preferred the time of new moon for their devotions. One of the principal stated festivals in the South Sea Islands—the *pae atna*—was held every three months. The Babylonians celebrate, with great magnificence, five days of the year. . .

"The people of Calabar were wont, on their Sabbath, to approach the Supreme Being (Avasi) in prayer. . . . . . The Ashantees, on their sacred day, worship their fetiches, and circumcise their children. . . . . . The Greeks and Romans, according to Aretius, consecrated Saturday to rest, conceiving it unfit for civil actions and warlike affairs, but suited for contemplation.

"The necessity of a weekly day of rest to the prosperity and even preservation of religion in the world has been proclaimed by the almost universal voice of mankind. Jews and Christians have ever elevated a seventh day to holy uses. Mohammedanism has always appropriated Friday to public devotion and instruction. Paganism, holding sacred in many instances the same proportion of time, has in no instance dropped all periodical festivals, till its people have well-nigh lost the conception of an object of worship. That so many, in regions and periods widely remote from each other, have observed a Sabbath, or some analogous arrangement, is a strong testimony to its religious necessity."—*The Sabbath Viewed in the Light of Reason, Revelation and History*, by James Gilfillan, pp. 359, 363, 200.

Mr. Cox remarks: "The hebdomadal revolution of time generally admitted in the world is also a great testimony to the original institution of the Sabbath. Of old it was catholic (universal) and is at present received among those nations whose converse was not begun until of late with any of those parts of the world where there is a light gone forth in these things from the

Scriptures. All nations, I say, in all ages, have from time immemorial made the revolution of seven days to be the first stated period of time. And this observance is still continued throughout the world, unless amongst them who in other things are openly degenerated from the law of nature; as those barbarous Indians, who have no computation of times, but by sleeps, moons, and winters. The measure of time by a day and night is pointed out to the sense by the diurnal course of the sun; lunar months, and solar years, are of an unavoidable observation unto all rational creatures. Whence, therefore, all men have reckoned time by days, months, and years, is obvious unto all. But whence the hebdomadal revolution, or weekly period of time should make its entrance, and obtain a catholic admittance, no man can give an account but with respect to some impressions on the minds of men from the constitution and law of our natures, with the tradition of a Sabbatical rest instituted from the foundation of the world."—*Works*, p. 278.

Calmet says: "Manasseh Ben Israel assures us that, according to the tradition of the ancients, Abraham and his posterity, having preserved the memory of creation, observed the Sabbath also in consequence of natural law to that purpose. It is also believed that the religion of the seventh day is preserved among the pagans; and that the observance of this day is as old as the world itself. Almost all the philosophers and poets acknowledge the seventh day holy."

The *Asiatic Journal* says: "The prime minister of the empire affirms that the Sabbath was anciently observed by the Chinese in conformity to the directions of the king."

Archbishop Usher says: "The very Gentiles, both civil and barbarous, both ancient and of later days, as it were by a *universal* kind of tradition, retained the distinction of the seventh day of the week."—*Works*, part i. chap. iv.

"The seventh day is sacred."—*Hesiod*. (B. C. 870.)

"Then came the seventh day that is sacred."—*Homer*. (B. C. 907.)

"It was the seventh day wherein all things were finished."—*Homer*. Linus says the same.

"Bad omens detained me on the sacred day of Saturn."—*Tibulus*.

"The sacredness of one of the seven days was generally admitted by all."

"Let it suffice, however, in a matter on which there is so general an agreement, to present the words of four eminent authors:—

"The septenary arrangement of days,' says Scaliger, 'was in use among the Orientals from the remotest antiquity.' 'We have reason to believe,' observes President de Goguet, 'that the institution of that period of seven days, called a week, was the first step taken by mankind in dividing and measuring their time. We find from time immemorial the use of this period among all nations, without any variation in the form of it. The Israelites, Assyrians, Egyptians, Indians, Arabians, and, in a word, all the nations of the East, have in all ages made use of a week consisting of seven days. We find the same custom among the ancient Romans, Gauls, Britons, Germans, the nations of the North, and of America.' According to Laplace, 'the week is perhaps the most ancient and incontestible monument of human knowledge.'" "It would appear that the Chinese, who have now no Sabbath, at one time honored the seventh day of the week."—*The Sabbath*, by Gilfillan, pp. 364, 365, 360.

By these testimonies, which might be extended to almost any length, we see that all nations in all ages have recognized and honored certain days, and most of them one day in seven, as sacred time. If any have not held a weekly sacred day, they have still had some holy days during the year which were sacred to their gods. All have their holidays, festival days, &c. How shall we account for this remarkable fact? It must have come either from a revelation or from nature. If from a revelation, it must have been given by God to the father of the race, from whom all have received it. This would be admitting all that we claim for the early origin of the Sabbath institution. Even then there must have been something in man's nature requiring such an institution in order to have perpetuated the memory and practice of it so long and so universally. But if this has sprung from the natural promptings of man's own nature, then it shows that the Sabbath precept, like all moral precepts, is founded upon a universal want of our race, and hence it is moral.

But it is further objected that the Sabbath institution is *partly* moral and *partly* ceremonial. It is moral so far as it relates to giving a certain day to God. Thus far there is a universal agreement of all nations. But it is ceremonial so far as it defines just what particular day or portion of time shall be kept holy. This, it is claimed, is proved by the fact that, by the light of nature alone, no man could possibly determine which day of the seven was the true Sabbath. It is asked, What is there in nature to distinguish the seventh day from the other days of the week? Nothing. Hence it is not so important which day we keep, provided that we keep one day in seven. But the same reasoning would prove that the first commandment was also partly moral and partly ceremonial. That men should worship some god is readily discerned by nature itself, and in this all have ever agreed. But just who is the true God, none can decide without a revelation. On this point there has been the greatest diversity. Some have chosen one as the true God and some another, till there are millions of different gods worshiped by men. This proves that it is immaterial *which* god you worship, provided you worship some one god! Who dare admit such a conclusion? Yet it is founded upon exactly the same mode of reasoning that is followed in arguing against a definite Sabbath day.

It is founded upon the false assumption that all moral principles are discoverable by the light of nature. We have already shown that this is not true in the case of the first commandment. Look at the second. "Thou shalt not make unto thee any graven image, or any likeness of anything that is in heaven above, or that is in the earth beneath, or that is in the water under the earth. Thou shalt not bow down thyself to them, nor serve them." All claim that this precept is moral in the highest sense. It forbids our making any thing to represent God and so worshiping him through his image. But this is just the thing that all nations who have had only the light of nature and reason to teach them have always thought was the most acceptable way to worship the Deity. Hence, with scarcely an exception, all men in all ages and nations have made and used images in worshiping their gods. Probably no other religious practice has been so universal as this. Indeed, notwithstanding all that God has said against this in the Bible, many of those who believe and reverence that book have been constantly inclined to do just what is here forbidden. Witness the Jews in the Old Testament, and the Catholics, Greeks, etc., in the gospel age. And this is done, too, with a religious sense of duty to God.

Here is a moral precept, then, which never has been discovered by the light of nature or reason. The best judgment of mankind, unaided by a revelation, has been directly opposed to this commandment. All heathen nations have used images, built magnificent temples to them, made rich offerings to them, made laws to protect them, and have considered it the highest sacrilege to molest them. If we had no better evidence from the light of nature and the general consent of mankind in favor of the fourth commandment, our opponents might well triumph over us from this standpoint.

Take the commandments against murder, adultery, stealing, and lying. We would suppose that the light of nature alone, without a revelation from God, would teach men that these things were wrong. But the history of the world proves that this is not the case. All these crimes have been tolerated, taught, practiced, and legalized in many of the wisest heathen nations. I have before me "Horne's Introduction," and "Leland's Revelation," in both which these learned men conclusively show the necessity of a divine revelation concerning the plainest moral principles.

They show that suicide, abortion, killing of weak or deformed infants, offering human beings in sacrifice to the gods, fornication, prostitution, and adultery, stealing, lying, &c., have all been generally practiced by the most enlightened heathen nations, and, by their wisest philosophers and lawgivers, defended as right, and according to nature and reason. The first of these eminent authors says:—

"Prostitution, in all its deformity, was systematically annexed to various pagan temples, was often a principal source of their revenues, and was, in some countries, even compulsory upon the female population. Other impurities were solemnly practiced by them in their temples and in public, from the very thought of which our minds revolt. Besides the numbers of men who were killed in the bloody sports and spectacles instituted in honor of their deities, human sacrifices were offered to propitiate them. Boys were whipped on the altar of Diana, sometimes till they died. How many lovely infants did the Carthaginians sacrifice to their implacable god, Moloch! What numbers of human victims, in times of public danger, did they immolate to appease the resentment of the offended deities!"— *Horne's Introduction*, vol. i. pp. 16, 17.

"Thus theft, as is well known, was permitted

in Egypt and in Sparta. Plato taught the expediency and lawfulness of exposing children in particular cases; and Aristotle, also of abortion. The exposure of infants, and the putting to death of children who were weak or imperfect in form, was allowed at Sparta by Lycurgus. At Athens, the great seat and nursery of philosophers, the women were treated and disposed of as slaves, and it was enacted that infants which appeared to be maimed, should either be killed or exposed."—*Id.*, p. 19.

"Truth was but of small account among many, even of the best heathens; for they taught that on many occasions *a lie was to be preferred to the truth* itself."

"Dr. Whitby has collected many maxims of the most eminent heathen sages, in corroboration of the fact above stated. The following examples are taken from his note on Eph. 4:25:—

"'A lie is better than a hurtful truth.'—*Menander*.

"'Good is better than truth.'—*Proclus*.

"'When telling a lie will be profitable, let it be told.'—*Darius, in Herodotus*, lib. iii. c. 62.

"'He may lie who knows how to do it in a suitable time.'—*Plato apud Stobæum*, Serm. 12.

"'There is nothing decorous in truth but when it is profitable. Yea, sometimes truth is hurtful, and lying is profitable to men.'—*Maximus Tyrius*, Diss. 3, p. 29;" *Id.*, p. 20.

To the same purpose, Mr. Leland remarks:—

"The custom of exposing weak and helpless children, which, one should think, is contrary to the most intimate feelings of humanity, obtained very generally among the most civilized nations; and yet they do not appear to have been sensible that in this they acted a wrong and inhuman part, but looked upon it to be a prudent and justifiable practice."—*Leland's Revelation*, vol. ii. p. 7.

Of the laws of Lycurgus, the wisest and best of all heathen lawgivers, the same author says:—

"There were common baths in which the men and women bathed together. And it was ordered that the young maidens should appear naked in the public exercises, as well as the young men, and that they should dance naked with them at the solemn festivals."—*Id.*, p. 46.

Plato, the prince of heathen philosophers, indorsed and recommended this custom! Upon this the above writer remarks:—

"A remarkable proof this, that the greatest men among the pagans, when left to their own judgments in matters of morality, were apt to form wrong notions concerning it, even in instances where one should think the dictates of nature and reason might have given them better directions."—*Note*, p. 47.

John Locke, the great Christian philosopher, says:—

"Whatever was the cause, it is evident in fact that human reason, unassisted, failed in its great and proper business of morality."—*Reasonableness of Christianity; in his Works*, vol. ii. p. 532.

Says Mr. Leland again:—

"Man appears from the frame of his nature to be a moral agent, and designed to be governed by a law. Accordingly, God hath given him a law to be the rule of his duty. The scheme of those who pretend that this law is naturally and necessarily known to all men without instruction is contrary to fact and experience. . . . When men fell from the right knowledge of God, they fell also in important instances from the right knowledge of moral duty."

"It appears, therefore, that what is called the moral sense was not designed to be an adequate guide in morals; nor is it, alone considered, and left merely to itself, fit to have the supreme direction as to the moral conduct."—Vol. ii. pp. 8, 15.

The *Christian Union* of Dec. 16, 1874, says:—

"Prof. Julius H. Seelye, of Amherst College, has been lecturing the past week before the Yale Divinity School on Missions. The course comprises six lectures, three of which remain to be given this week. The first lecture was upon the condition and needs of the unchristian world. He presented a vivid picture of the degradation of these nations, based not merely on his own observation, which has been extensive, but supporting his statements by reference to authorities accessible to all. China, as one of the most promising of pagan nations, and whose civilization has been so widely lauded, was shown to be most shockingly corrupt in its social and private life. Lying, insincerity, licentiousness, and almost every vice mentioned in Scripture, is practiced without restraint. Their virtue is entirely external. India is in a similar condition. Before the establishment of the English in that country, not less than ten thousand infants were put to death by their parents per month in the single province of Bengal. This condition is true not only of modern half-civilized pagans, but it is found where civilization has shown some of its most renowned trophies. In Greece and Rome, society was all pollution. The most classic writings reveal it. Even their philosophers taught the most unmentionable vices. The first chapter of Romans is not an untrue portraiture of pagan corruption."

The foregoing arguments and facts conclusively show that it is no evidence that a precept is not moral simply because the light of nature alone does not clearly point it out. It further shows that when we appeal to the common consent of mankind, we find just as general a recognition of the principle of the Sabbath precept as we do of any of the other moral precepts. Hence this objection is not a valid one.

OBJ. II. *All moral duties and precepts are equally obligatory at all times; but the Sabbath precept makes an act wrong if done upon one day which would be right if done upon any other day. Therefore, it is not a moral precept.*

Our opponents ask, "Would adultery, lying, stealing, &c., be wrong upon one day but allowable all the rest of the week? Can an act be morally wrong at one time, which would not be at another? What is there in the nature of the day itself which makes the seventh day any different from other days? Is it not naturally just like other days?" In answer, we affirm that there are many acts which are morally wrong at one time but right at another time. A works for B at ten shillings per day for ten hours. At noon A has one hour during which he can eat, rest, sleep, or do what he pleases. But if A should idle around one hour during working hours he would be defrauding B and thus committing a moral wrong. Again, D borrows $100 of E and pledges his word and gives his note to pay that money to E one year from date. Now D has a moral right to keep and use that money through the whole year till the last day, pay day, comes. But if he keeps it beyond that day, then he is guilty of a moral wrong.

So innumerable cases might be cited where it would be morally wrong to do a thing at one time which would be right at another time. A couple are engaged to be married upon a set day. Now, entering upon certain relations before they are married would be grossly immoral; but the same relations after marriage would not be wrong. Is it said that the morality or immorality of the act is not because of anything inherent in the nature of the time itself, but because of a violation of an arbitrary agreement or law made concerning the time? Thus: A's act of resting during working hours would not be wrong if he had not agreed to work at that hour. Nor would D do wrong in not paying the $100 at the end of the year, if he had not promised to do it then. Very well; then an agreement or law can make an act immoral at one time which is moral at another time. This is sufficient to overthrow the objection.

But the seventh day is different from all other days. The other six days of the week came into being as working days, the Creator working upon them. But the seventh day first came into being under very different circumstances. All the earth and everything upon it was finished. All was beautiful, peaceful, and quiet. God then honored that day by resting upon it in celebration of creation finished. He then blessed and sanctified it. Gen. 2:1-3. Thus, from its very birth, this day has differed from all other days. A man has seven sons. Six were born in England, the seventh in America. The first six are Englishmen, the seventh is an American. In one sense they are all alike; but in another, they are not. The last is honored with being eligible to the highest office in our government, while the others never can be. So the first six days were working days; Eze. 46:1; Ex. 20:11; but the seventh was born a Sabbath day. Gen. 2:1-3. This difference between the days exists in the nature of things, and must always continue to exist.

But another fact, which we have purposely passed over until now, fully answers the objection we are considering. Moral precepts, it is said, are equally obligatory at all times; but the Sabbath precept applies to only one day in seven. This is a mistake. That precept, like all moral laws, covers all the time. It directs what we shall do upon the first six days as plainly as it does what we shall do upon the seventh day. "Six days shalt thou labor, and do all thy work; but the seventh day is the Sabbath of the Lord thy God; in it thou shalt not do any work." It will be seen that this commandment covers the whole week, directing what we shall do each day—how we shall use the time which God has given us. So it is not true that it applies only to one day out of seven.

Seeing that the Creator has given to us all our time, "life, and breath, and all things," Acts 17:25, has he not a moral right to direct how we shall use this time? Is it not highly reasonable that he should? Does nature teach us that we should fear and serve our Creator? So all claim, and so we believe. Does it not, then, also teach us that our Maker would care how we use our time? This is just as natural as that we should serve him at all. Indeed, it is implied in it; for serving God is an act, and it takes *time* to perform an act. Therefore, if nature teaches that men should serve God, it teaches that God is interested as to how men use their time. Hence, it is naturally to be expected that God would give directions concerning it. This is just what he has done in the fourth commandment. Therefore, that precept, like all moral laws, is reasonable and natural, and hence moral.

Obj. III. *The seventh day cannot be kept in all parts of the world. Therefore, it is not a moral institution.*

1. It is claimed that at the north pole there are several weeks when the sun does not set at all; and again there are weeks when it is dark all the time. How can the seventh day be distinguished and kept there?

If nature in this case proves anything, it proves that God never designed men to live there. First, there is nothing for men to do there, nothing to call them there but the love of adventure. Secondly, nature has made no provision to sustain a population there. At the nearest point to the north pole which men have been able to reach, all is a dreary, barren field of solid ice, except for a few weeks, and then only a few berries grow. Thirdly, most of those who have endeavored to reach the north pole have perished in the attempt. So an appeal to nature does not help the objector in this case.

But frequently those who raise this objection are strict observers of Sunday, the first day of the week. If there is any force in this objection, it comes with equal weight against Sunday-keeping. How can they keep the first day there? If they can find the first day, cannot we find the seventh? If they can keep Sunday, cannot we keep the Sabbath? But there is no trouble in either case. The days of the week are plainly marked there as well as here. Read the travels of Drs. Kane, Hall, and others who have been there. Did they experience any difficulty in keeping the reckoning of the days? None, whatever. The days are marked off by the revolutions of the earth, which are there, as well as here, indicated by the position of the sun. The most of the year, the sun rises and sets there the same as here; that is, as far north as men have ever penetrated. So far, there is no difficulty, of course. In mid-summer, for a short time, the sun is above the horizon all the time. Being so far north, a person can see the sun in its entire circuit around the earth, day and night. But it is easy to tell when it is overhead at noon, when it is going down in the west, when it is directly underneath at midnight, or when it is rising in the east in the morning. Can we not tell the time of day here by the position of the sun in the heavens without seeing it rise and set? Certainly. Then if we could see it all the way around, could we not tell just as well as when we see it only part of the way around? Of course; and so those testify who have been in the Arctic regions.

The following is from the description of a scene witnessed in the north of Norway, from a cliff one thousand feet above the sea:—

"The ocean stretched away in silent vastness at our feet; the sound of the waves scarcely reached our airy lookout; away in the north the huge old sun swung low along the horizon. We stood silent, looking at our watches. When both hands came together at twelve, midnight, the full round orb hung triumphantly above the wave; a bridge of gold running due north spanned the water between us and him. There he shone in silent majesty that knew no setting. .... In half an hour the sun had swung by perceptibly, the colors changed to those of morning, a fresh breeze rippled over the flood, one songster after another piped up in the grove behind us—we had slid into another day."

The change of the day, then, can be discerned even though the sun can be seen all the time.

But how is it in the winter when it is night for weeks together? I believe there is no time that rays of light cannot be seen in the south at noon of each day. This would be sufficient to mark each day. But the revolution of the earth can be as plainly and as easily told by the position of the stars at night as it can by the sun at day. Any one accustomed to observing the stars knows this. They appear to rise and set and to go around the earth the same as the sun. Indeed, astronomers always reckon the day by the stars. Read the following letter which I received from an eminent astronomer touching this point:—

"Ogden, Utah, Sept. 24, 1873.

"Eld. D. M. Canright: By observations of the stars, the time can be found out at any time, day or night. Knowing the time at which any star ought to be in the meridian, we find the difference between noon and the observing time, or the local time. Stars being visible in the daytime and at night, on all places of the earth, it is possible to determine the time without seeing the sun.

"(Signed,) Dr. F. Kampf,
"*Astronomer of the U. S. corps of Engineers.*"

So, then, the exact time of day can be told by the stars, and they can be seen in the absence of the sun. Hence this objection is without foundation.

2. The earth is round. When it is noon here, it is midnight in China. A person traveling around the earth in an easterly direction will gain a day, while another going around it in a westerly direction will lose a day. This shows that the same definite day cannot be kept all around the world. So says the objector.

It is remarkable that most of those who urge this as a difficulty in our way, do themselves claim to keep the first day of the week holy, in honor of the resurrection of Jesus, which occurred on the other side of our earth. How can they keep the same first day all around the earth? Is the earth round on Saturday and flat on Sunday? If there is any difficulty in the case, then it is just as much against keeping one day as another. Therefore, those who hold to the observance of any day should never urge this objection against the Sabbath.

When God made this round earth he also made man to dwell on all the face of it; Gen. 1:28; Acts 17:26; and at the same time he made the

Sabbath for man. Gen. 2:1-3; Mark 2:27. God would not require an impossibility, hence all men can keep it. So we find that they do keep it without any such difficulty as this objection supposes. The Jews, who are scattered in every part of the earth and all around it, keep the seventh-day Sabbath. Starting from Palestine, some have come around the world *via* Europe and the Atlantic Ocean. Others have come *via* Asia, China, and the Pacific Ocean. Both have met in America keeping the same day. There is no disagreement among them in any part of the world. This demonstrates that men can travel all around this earth and still keep the same day.

Those who keep Sunday live in all parts of the earth, and have traveled all around it both ways. Do they find any difficulty in keeping the first day? Not in the least. This objection is all imaginary; for, practically, no one ever had any such trouble. Seventh-day Adventists and Seventh-day Baptists are scattered nearly around the globe; and yet they find no difficulty in keeping the seventh-day Sabbath.

The facts are these: The day begins at sunset. Gen. 1:5; Lev. 23:32; Mark 1:32. When the sun sets Friday evening in Asia, then the seventh-day Sabbath begins there. A few hours later the sun sets in Europe. Then the Sabbath has come there. Still later it sets in New York; and now the Sabbath has come there. Three hours later, the sun sets in California; and now the seventh day has arrived here. When the seventh day is in Asia, then those living there can observe it; when it comes to Europe, then those there can keep it; and when it gets around here to America, then we can keep it. It is exactly the same day when it comes to America that it was when it started in Asia, though it comes here later. A train of cars starts from Chicago at seven o'clock Monday morning and arrives at Omaha five hundred miles west of that city the next morning at the same hour. Is it not the same train that started from Chicago twenty-four hours before? Certainly. Suppose that this is train No. 7. A business man in Chicago has several hired men scattered all along the road between Chicago and Omaha. He orders them all to take train No. 7, which leaves Chicago at seven Monday morning, and meet him at Omaha. Would all these men go down to their different depots at seven Monday morning to take train No. 7? They would not find it there if they did. But each one waits till the train arrives at his place, and then he gets aboard, and the last one would get on about twenty-four hours later than the first one. But would it not be the same train, No. 7, that started in Chicago? Of course it would.

The Lord commands his servants all around the world to keep the seventh day. Each one is to keep it when it comes where he is, not when it comes where some one else is. When it comes to those in Asia, they can keep it. Several hours later, it comes to England, and then they keep it, and so on around the world.

This is sufficient to show that there is no such difficulty as this objection supposes. For a full answer to it, the reader is referred to a tract by Eld. J. N. Andrews, entitled, "The Definite Seventh Day," for sale at the *Review Office*, Battle Creek, Mich., and at the office of the *Signs of the Times*, Oakland, Cal.

OBJ. IV. *Nature keeps no Sabbath.*

It is said that all the operations of nature go on just the same upon the seventh day as upon other days. Birds and beasts keep no Sabbath; it rains and snows, the sun shines, water runs, grass grows, &c., &c., upon that day as upon others. Hence nature teaches no Sabbath.

Answer. This objection is founded upon an entire misapprehension of the design of the Sabbath. "The Sabbath was made for man," the same as were the other moral laws. He needs it and can be benefited by it. Inanimate nature neither feels, thinks, nor reasons; hence it needs no Sabbath. The animals which do not labor need no rest-day. They are not capable of worshiping God, and hence need no day for that purpose. They cannot appreciate God's power and authority as Creator, and therefore need no sign to remind them of it. But the commandment does provide rest for all working animals.

The same mode of reasoning would set aside all the commandments. Thus, neither fish, fowls, nor beasts, worship God. Neither does water, fire, grass, nor trees. Therefore men should not worship him! It is a remarkable fact that every thrust against God's Sabbath strikes with equal force against the other moral commandments, showing that they are inseparably bound together. Take another commandment: "Thou shalt not commit adultery." None of the animals below man regard this precept, but they have promiscuous intercourse. Shall men, therefore, appeal to nature, and practice the same? Once more: "Thou shalt not kill." Beasts regard not the lives of their fellows. Shall we appeal to this fact to show that this command is not founded in nature? Certainly, if we go to the same witnesses for proof against the Sabbath. Again: "Honor thy father and thy mother." Beasts pay no regard to this precept. As soon as they are grown, they forget all relations and treat all alike.

Therefore an appeal to the practice of dumb animals and inanimate nature will not help the case of our no-Sabbath opponents unless they are prepared to go against all moral laws. Thus we have answered all the objections urged against the position that the Sabbath is a moral precept. We believe that it has been fully and clearly shown that the Sabbath deserves a place in the the moral law, and that God did not make a mistake in placing it there.

THE IMPORTANCE OF THE SABBATH.

From the foregoing we see that the Sabbath is an institution of the greatest importance to man physically, mentally, morally, and spiritually. It has been plainly shown that men absolutely need such a day of rest from physical or mental labor. The man who does not obey this law of nature, sins against himself, and will inevitably suffer loss in the end. The social benefits of the Sabbath in promoting friendly intercourse, moral culture, and refinement of manners, are beyond all estimation even if only this life is considered.

But it is in the holy work of religion, in man's duties to his Creator, that the highest importance of the Sabbath is seen. It sets apart a definite, regular, and oft-recurring day of rest from all worldly employments, upon which men can be free to attend to the worship of God. No other law can compare in importance with the Sabbath in preserving and promoting the knowledge and worship of the true God. We have seen that it is the sign which distinguishes the true God from all false gods. It is the memorial of the great work of creation. It is the seal to the moral law of Jehovah, without which, that law would be of no authority. This fact alone elevates the

Sabbath precept in importance above any other. We have seen that the Sabbath is a moral precept in every sense of the term. Every argument against it falls with equal weight against one or more of the other commandments of the moral law.

Our great and constant danger is that we shall become "choked with cares and riches and pleasures of this life;" Luke 8:14: and so bear no fruit for the Lord. To obviate this, the Lord has interposed the Sabbath after six days of labor, to break up the tide of worldliness and call man's attention back to God. If it were not for this provision, the business of the world would absorb all man's attention, and God would soon be forgotten. Man needs a constant reminder of his duty to God, an oft-recurring test of his own spiritual condition. For this purpose, no other precept is like the Sabbath.

We have before shown that the principle involved in the violation of all the other commandments is also involved in the violation of the Sabbath. A man covets his neighbor's property. This leads him to steal it. So a man covets God's time for his own work; hence he proceeds to take it and use it for himself, and he thus robs God. A man who will knowingly and deliberately use God's holy day for his own worldly, selfish purposes, would also steal if he could do it with the same impunity. If a man will steal from his Creator, will he not from his fellowmen? I know that men do not like to regard it in this light, but it is true, notwithstanding. When we come to look at the claims and sacredness of the Sabbath day in a proper light, it must be seen that it is no slight offense to disregard the Sabbath. I cannot conceive how a man could set at naught God's authority in so defiant a manner as this. Look at the facts a moment. The omnipotent God, whose glory fills all Heaven, whose hands have made the universe, has created our earth, ourselves, and every blessing which we enjoy. To commemorate this great work he has set apart, as sacred to himself, the Sabbath day. With a voice that shook the earth, he has forbidden us to use this day in doing our own work. With a full knowledge of these facts before him, with the law of God pointing out his duty, with the eyes of Jehovah upon him, a man arises Sabbath morning and deliberately proceeds to use this holy time in his own business. How must such an act appear in the eyes of God? How will it appear on the record in the Judgment? What act could puny man perform which would more deliberately set at naught the law and authority of the great Creator? Reader, we beseech you to stop and think seriously of this matter, and consider whether the observance of the Sabbath is not of greater importance than you have hitherto considered it.

On several important occasions when God wished especially to test the people touching their loyalty to him, he has chosen the Sabbath as best adapted to this purpose. The children of Israel, during their long sojourn in Egypt, had largely apostatized from God. Before the Lord would entrust them with his law, he tested them to see whether they would respect it or not. Thus he says: "Behold, I will rain bread from heaven for you; and the people shall go out and gather a certain rate every day, that I may prove them, whether they will walk in my law, or no." Ex. 16:4. How does he prove them? He selects the Sabbath for that purpose. See Ex. 16:23-29.

The Lord gave them manna from heaven six days, and commanded them to prepare twice as much on the sixth day as on other days; and told them not to go out on the seventh day. But they hearkened not to the Lord, which brought from the Lord this sharp rebuke: "How long refuse ye to keep my commandments and my laws?" But they refused and rebelled, time after time, till the Lord sware that he would destroy them in the wilderness. Their continued violation of the Sabbath was one of the chief reasons why God shut them out of the promised land, and slew them in the wilderness. This fact is plainly stated by Ezekiel, chap. 20:12, 13.

On another occasion, just before the Babylonish captivity, when the people had become very corrupt and disobedient, God made to them this remarkable proposition: "It shall come to pass, if ye diligently hearken unto me, saith the Lord, to bring in no burden through the gates of this city on the Sabbath day, but hallow the Sabbath day, to do no work therein; then shall there enter into the gates of this city kings and princes sitting upon the throne of David, riding in chariots and on horses, they, and their princes, the men of Judah, and the inhabitants of Jerusalem; and this city shall remain forever." Jer. 17:19-25.

Upon this remarkable passage Justin Edwards remarks: "This is true. A man who will conscientiously and sacredly observe the Sabbath day will not have a heart to commit any other crime. In the above passage the Lord shows his appreciation of the Sabbath by placing the Sabbath in the light he has." Fearing they would not obey him, the Lord added this warning: "But if ye will not hearken unto me to hallow the Sabbath day, and not to bear a burden, even entering in at the gates of Jerusalem on the Sabbath day; then will I kindle a fire in the gates thereof, and it shall devour the palaces of Jerusalem, and it shall not be quenched." Verse 27. But they did not obey him nor keep his Sabbath day, and therefore he sent them into captivity. 2 Chron. 36:16, 17.

That the violation of the Sabbath was one of the chief reasons for which God sent them into captivity, is thus confessed by Nehemiah when he found some of them again breaking the Sabbath after their return. He says: "Then I contended with the nobles of Judah, and said unto them, What evil thing is this that ye do, and profane the Sabbath day? Did not your fathers thus, and did not our God bring all this evil upon us, and upon this city? Yet ye bring more wrath upon Israel by profaning the Sabbath." Neh. 13:17, 18. A proper consideration of the above passage will give us some idea of how important the Sabbath is in the estimation of God.

Again, when the Lord calls the Gentiles to serve him he makes to them this promise: "Also the sons of the stranger, that join themselves to the Lord, to serve him, and to love the name of the Lord, to be his servants, every one that keepeth the Sabbath from polluting it, and taketh hold of my covenant; even them will I bring to my holy mountain." Isa. 56:6. Obedience to the Sabbath is the thing named by the Lord as the condition of their acceptance with him. Would God have accepted them if they had gone on worshiping idols, murdering, coveting, stealing, etc.? Of course not; and yet the Lord does not mention any of these things, but simply says if they will keep his Sabbath, he will accept them. The reason is that the Sabbath is a testing truth. All others are implied in it. If they would keep the Sabbath, they would obey him in other things.

At another time the Lord made this proposition to the Jews: "If thou turn away thy foot from the Sabbath, from doing thy pleasure on my holy day; and call the Sabbath a delight, the holy of the Lord, honorable; and shalt honor him, not doing thine own ways, nor finding thine own pleasure, nor speaking thine own words; then shalt thou delight thyself in the Lord; and I will cause thee to ride upon the high places of the earth, and feed thee with the heritage of Jacob thy father; for the mouth of the Lord hath spoken it." Isa. 58:13, 14. What a wonderful promise this was, and yet the one condition named is that of obedience to the Sabbath. Thus it will be seen that on many occasions the Lord has chosen the Sabbath precept as the one by which to test the people. Is it anything remarkable, then, that in these last days, when the people have apostatized from God, the Lord should again bring up his holy Sabbath as a testing truth by which to prepare a people for translation? To us it seems very reasonable.

Finally, obedience to the Sabbath converts men to God in other respects. Our opponents find fault with us because we urge the Sabbath so strongly. They represent us as preaching that if a man will only keep the Sabbath it is all he need do to be saved. This is false, as all know who are acquainted with our teachings. We teach that men must obey all the law of God, repent of their sins, and believe in Jesus Christ for their remission. But we have found by a long experience that the man who will conscientiously keep the Sabbath will also keep all God's commandments. Indeed, before a man decides to step out in opposition to almost everybody, and sacredly observe the Sabbath of the Lord, he must decide in his own mind to give up the world and become a servant of the Lord. Hence, we have found that almost invariably, however wicked a man has been before, as soon as he commences the observance of the Sabbath, he also commences to be a praying, Bible-reading, God-fearing man. This is only a legitimate result of Sabbath-keeping, as we have previously shown. On the other hand, those who will not keep the Sabbath day seldom obey God in anything else. With all these facts before us, we appeal to the reader's judgment and conscience to decide whether or not the Sabbath is of so little importance as its opponents are wont to represent it. Is it not, on the other hand, the key-stone of God's great moral law, without which the law would have no strength to stand? Dear reader, as you value your soul and the favor of your Creator, do not pass by the light which God in his providence is now causing to shine out so clearly upon the subject of his holy but down-trodden Sabbath day. May the Lord help you to turn away your feet from the Sabbath, and call it "a delight, the holy of the Lord, honorable."

I Was Canright's Secretary
Carrie Johnson's story forms a new and fascinating portrait of Dudley Marvin Canright.

Meek & Mighty— The Man Moses
Through the writings of E. G. White, readers can follow the life of this extraordinary man.

Other Titles from TEACH Services, Inc.

Dare to Be a Daniel
E. G. White expounds upon the life of this Biblical hero, Daniel, showing the lessons that can be learned as this man lived his life to honor and serve God.

Nehemiah– Restoring the Breach
The 1904 Southern Watchman articles by E. G. White, dealing with the work of Nehemiah, are reproduced here in their entirety.

We'd love to have you download our catalog of
titles we publish at:

www.TEACHServices.com

or write or email us your thoughts,
reactions, or criticism about this
or any other book we publish at:

TEACH Services, Inc.
254 Donovan Road
Brushton, NY 12916

info@TEACHServices.com

or you may call us at:

518/358-3494

Produced in partnership with
LNFBooks.com